A PLACE IN THE SKY

A PLACE IN THE SKY

The Story of an Irish Airline Pilot

by

AIDAN QUIGLEY

THE MERCIER PRESS

DUBLIN and CORK

THE MERCIER PRESS

4 Bridge Street, Cork

25 Lower Abbey Street, Dublin 1

© Aidan Quigley, 1974

ISBN 0 85342 412 8

To Stephanie – in gratitude; and to all the pilots, hostesses and engineers of Aer Lingus, past and present, with whom I have been privileged to work and fly.

ACKNOWLEDGEMENTS

I wish to acknowledge the use of statistics and summaries obtained from the following sources:

An Foras Forbartha.

The Department of Transport and Power – Aeronautical Branch.

Aer Lingus.

The British Civil Aviation Authority.

The International Civil Aviation Organisation.

The Irish Airline Pilots Association.

By kind permission of:

Mr. P. Conran

Colonel W. P. Delemere

Captain J. C. Kelly-Rogers

Mr. H. McCabe

Commandant F. O'Connor

I availed of information on Irish aviation which they had published in the Irish Defence Journal – *An Cosantoir*. Mr. H. McCabe was especially helpful.

I

The big jet was heavy with fuel, and as we trundled slowly out of the parking area at New York, a portion of the taxiway undulated and the Boeing rode gently up and down like a porpoise. The ground controller called on the radio: 'Hold it there Irish. Let Alitalia pass first.' We moved in behind the DC8 and followed until it stopped on the taxiway parallel to the runway. I switched off the lights, applied the parking brake, and we peered intently into the night.

Pulsating anticollision lights, blue taxi lights, red obstruction lights, fixed landing lights and nose wheel lights all extended in a semicircle ahead until they lost their individuality in the darkness.

Away to the left the long windowed shadow of a commuter train ran along the placid waters of Jamacia Bay.

A sudden brilliance projected our Boeing onto the pavement ahead as a monstrous moving thing on stilts. The fantasy grew larger and more grotesque, rising high off the ground and doubling back upon its parent, until Scandanavian Flight 412 came to a standstill behind and switched off his lights. My co-pilot had undone his tie and the glistening beads of perspiration on his forehead were matched by those that ran down my nose; the temperature was even higher in the passenger cabin. Alitalia began rolling, so I released the brakes and came up behind him. The controller kept the line moving until we were in position near the runway.

The Swiss, Dutch and British jets ahead were heavy, and in our cockpit the mounting roar of their engines was audible as the pilots held the brakes and allowed the power to build. The full throat of the Rolls Royce was a different sound from that of the others, and it came as a crackle which vibrated our cockpit. Eager and fast went many of those American aeroplanes, but heavy and slow went the Europeans, the beam of their lights bouncing with the nose wheels. The European run was protracted, and their body angle low as they left the ground and pushed slowly into the night; their lights faded one by one and the exhaust smoke dissipated across the runway and over Jamaica Bay. We lined up and followed them into the darkness.

We flew on up the airways at 30,000 feet and watched a watermelon moon lying down below on the clouds near the horizon. Control called to warn of opposite direction traffic 2000 feet above. Searching the sky we found his navigation lights; I flicked on the landing lights and he made a friendly reply. Fifty miles later we entered an area of turbulence. I switched on the seat belt sign and made an announcement to our passengers. As the heaving got worse we strapped on full safety harness. The third pilot adjusted the power and activated the engine ignitors, guarding against interruption of the smooth burning flow of kerosene and a possible flameout. It was a clear night and the turbulence was coming from a very strong wind, a wind that was rapidly changing its flight pattern both in direction and depth over a small zone. We could hear the 'whoosh' of the rushing air varying its sound pattern as its fury rose and fell. I glanced out of the side window to watch the wingtip beyond waggling up and down. The red reflection from the overhead anti-collision beacon was ignoring the turbulence and dancing across its polished surface.

We were in the stuff about 20 minutes when it abated as suddenly as it had begun, and the wind speed dropped from 180 knots to a mere 60. We were now floating alone beneath the countless stars. The navigator swivelled the periscopic sextant into position, and the third pilot, having reset the engine power, peacefully munched on a large New York tuna fish 'special'.

The cockpit of a Boeing 707 is superbly designed for vision, and that night the moon was well up over Newfoundland with many stars for company. Whole fistfuls of them were painted in the window sets, and each time the aeroplane banked a fresh scene was formed on the canvas. Our front windows were full and Venus rising rapidly out of the east added changing colour as she moved through the sky. Ocean clouds gleamed far below, and through the rifts could be glimpsed 20 lights on the water — cod-fishermen out at the Newfoundland Banks. The Northern Lights were weaving and part of the halo had slipped away from its source and drifted to the south in ghostly suspension. But it was the moon that dominated the spectacle and flooded that magnificent stage with a strange intensity, as we in our little metal particle drifted across the roof of the world. There was a brief alien movement in the star pattern as a lonely satellite sailed across our field of vision. The moon passed us on its way as we flew east through the night.

Ocean Station Charlie is a cutter of the United States Coastguard, permanently steaming in position 52 degrees 45 minutes north latitude and 33 degrees 30 minutes west longitude. It is one of a chain of similar vessels which give navigational assistance and weather information to overflying aircraft and provide search and rescue facilities for both aircraft and ships.

The cutter was below, steaming at half speed ahead to keep in place against the rising northwesterly gale. The radio beacon was correctly coding 'On Station' as the vessel was accurately manoeuvred in the gale to maintain its position.

We called the ship for a radar fix, and a small white light on the radio panel of the Boeing winked intermittently as the radar operator on the ocean station signalled.

'Shamrock 104, I have a fix. Are you ready to copy?'

the routine transmission began. When it was complete the operator asked us if he could be of any further service to us. 'Negative,' I replied, 'but we have a message for you, standby.'

I depressed the button on my microphone and held it near the co-pilot who proceeded to deliver the 'Irish Washer Woman' in his own impeccable style on tin whistle. His crystal notes trickled into 'Charlie's' radio room and echoed louder as the operator turned up his volume. The blue-green light of the ship's radar scope must have provided an unusual background when the melody of the jig cascaded around the crewmen. The co-pilot went straight into the 'Rakes of Mallow', but the notes were becoming intermittent as the call of the tin whistle wafted towards Shannon at 600 knots.

One hundred and twenty miles from Shannon we closed the throttles and lowered the nose to keep a speed of 260 knots. Dipping down toward the white puffy cloud tops, the aeroplane sped along until it burst through the mass and lost its identity, becoming enveloped in the grey amorphous swirl. We broke through the overcast approaching the mouth of the Shannon to find all of Dingle and Cahirciveen and Kenmare wrapped in slumber. The coast stood out, the sea was calm and the beauty of the place was revealed in splendour as we flew to the east. There was mist over the mountains of Kerry, but further to the north the Galway hills were clear, and the flat barren outline of the Aran Islands was visible in the waters near the far shores of rocky Clare.

Soon we were on the runway at Shannon and taxying in towards the terminal building. I shut the engines down, the co-pilot opened his side window, and the fresh sweet morning air of Ireland filled the cockpit.

II

The Foxford where I grew up in the 1930's was a haven of prosperity in an otherwise depressed area. The town possessed a woollen mill and two schools, both national and convent. There was even the sophistication of a music academy.

The wages in the factory were good, and were paid in a differential scheme. In practice this meant that two men could do precisely the same work at a loom, but the man with a wife and family would earn more than the bachelor. At Christmas those employees who needed it received blankets or suitlengths of tweed or serge from the mill. It was a system which catered for the needs of this country town, as Ireland and Foxford with her emerged from the twilight of the unwanted imperial marriage to mother her two new children: national freedom and industrial enlightenment.

Foxford had been a designated 'black potato' area; the blight came regularly and destroyed the crop. Land was poor and unfruitful and the only possessions apart from poteen and talk were an abundance of turf and water. However, while nature could not provide comfortable living conditions the Irish Sisters of Charity could. At the turn of the century they came to this small town, or village, as it was then. They built their woollen factory on the river bank just below the Moy Bridge. There the mill race fed the turbines with a swift flow of energy in bounteous supply.

The waters as we knew them then tumbled and cascaded over half a mile of rough riverbed below the bridge until, their vigour dissipated, they ran through the eel weirs and spread out to a deep and flowing river. It ribboned its way down the Green and around a small island or two and then, as if it had a sense of intelligence in realising its strength was spent, it gathered itself in slow majesty to flow with easy grace and generous sweeps through the ten miles to Ballina.

Nature, which had been so cruel to its people in providing sustenance, relented in endowing the land with a rugged and majestic beauty. Nephin mountain was to the west where it heaved itself almost three thousand feet into the sky; its symmetrical shape stood behind Lough Conn and Cullin. In the long winters it scowled when misty rain clung to its majestic head, or when rolling grey clouds buffeted its mass. But on a summer's day it stood like an Egyptian pyramid in bright and proud relief, jealously guarding the beauty of its lakes and yawning with soft pleasure in the warmth of the sun.

Pontoon on Lough Cullin was a focal point of nature's artistry, and the 'Angler's Rest' was its centre-piece. This hotel was set between Granny Healy's garden of rhododendron bushes and shrubs and the rising ground towards the road to Corriosla. The 'Angler's Rest' faced the rush cluttered bay already invaded too deeply by sand, the boat slip was over to the left, and the full panorama of the lough was dotted with rocks; those that lay beneath the surface were known in size and depth to every gillie.

They were all fishermen in Foxford, the young and the old, and whilst most of them tried their luck from the picturesque foam flecked pools of the weirs or the silent water down the Green, the dedicated plied the long waters to the lakes. The men that fished from the bridge or the falls were never to be seen up the town or down the Green. Each had a time to fish; some early in the morning before work, others late at night. The professionals used the handmade fly, but the majority picked their bait from the rocks as required or stocked it away the day before in a nail pricked cocoa tin. Many stretches of water were privately owned, and salmon were acquired by a variety of methods; simple fishing, netting, or other less orthodox but more rewarding techniques.

As in any rural community the people in Foxford knew everything of each other. News was eagerly received, relished, digested, and finally passed on to the next suffering little in the telling. Every pattern of behaviour was known and felt, and each daily sight or sound conveyed not only a meaning but a character. A member of the community had a role to fill, no matter how small. The opening or closing of doors, the clamour of cows coming down the street, the tone of a car horn and the way it was blown, the tremolo whistle, the half known song, the noisy bicycle, the barking dog, the rattling trap, the laughing lilt of a woman's voice, the metallic clank of the pump; all of these noises were part of the life and roles of the people, and an absence or an irregularity within the pattern was an indication of something wrong.

Foxford was a typical Mayo town and turf was the common fuel. There were brown stains on the gable ends of the houses, stains which grew over the years as the tarry deposits from the turf smoke seeped through the walls and lifted the plaster into round brown moulds. Like every other small boy I knew each stain as I knew the precise number of telephone cables on the poles. On many a day I watched in fascination from my bedroom window as the water droplets gathered pendulously on the lines near the insulators; they grew fat by feeding on their neighbours and then, with pear distended bellies and a tenuous elongated connection to the wire, they slid down the incline from the cup finally losing their grip to tumble and burst on the roadway below.

On a fair day the only area where cow dung did not drop was the footpath near the convent; planks were placed on tar barrels to keep the animals away. Everywhere else from the mill to the top of the town, cattle jammed the street from an early hour. Here and there on the pavement a special calf was displayed in a creel or a crudely made pen. Sows grunted underfoot and squealed disapproval when potential buyers poked them too enthusiastically.

Down near the pump the gathering thinned out to herds of sheep and goats and here the latecomers had a last free space where they could gather momentum before plunging into the brown and white mass to buy and to sell. Their cattle ran with them and incredibly found a position where none seemed possible. The ritual of bargaining was carried out to the fullest; hand clasps, spits, swears, walking away in a refusal only to return and negotiate again, until finally the luck penny was argued out.

In the market square were the 'Cheap Jacks' standing by their canopied lorries with fall away sides. With all the vigour of Arab traders they sold secondhand clothes, pots and pans, delph, statues, lamps, glasses, Japanese vases, holy water fonts, brushes, clocks, and chow dog mantlepiece ornaments. It was all there and the sing-song voices which accompanied it offered a free set of six plates with every purchase over a pound.

There were many pubs in Foxford and with them as many businesses. Shops that had long since ceased to sell liquor in any quantity held onto the licence and kept the permit valid. Some had a grocery counter on one side with the bar on the other, and the 'snug' was warm and inviting, with bags of meal and sides of bacon surrounding the customers. In the drapery shops the inevitable small mahogany counter was tucked away into a corner at the back. Normal business had ceased in many, but the nominality of the licence was maintained by a few bottles of whiskey and sherry scattered on the dusty shelves. The most famous of all was an establishment where the enterprising proprietor made it possible to order your coffin over a pint.

In 1933 I went to a secondary school at the Cistercian Abbey, Roscrea. The country around the monastery was fertile as it abounded in the past with the estates of the landowners who had acquired plantations during the Elizabethan and Cromwellian rule. I well remember the school outings which took us to these places. The desmesnes we visited were full of stories, hushed whisperings of Cromwell's soldiers and Irish gentry; but they were peopled now by elderly spinsters, retired colonels, eccentrics, and all the leftovers of a by-gone age. The mansions had slipped into decay, the ornamental pools were choked with weed, and the large conservatories were badly in need of paint and glass. The once shrub-lined paths had fused quietly back into nature. Over it all lay the eerie uncanny twilight air, damp in the winter gloom, and full of ghostly tales of happenings long ago.

The Cistercian monk is a contemplative, but manual labour is an important part of his daily routine. The abbot would lead the priests and brothers into the fields to dig or weed, no doubt an excellent physical exercise, but it humbled the man and made all equal. The work at the monastery centred on farming, and with it the diverse and allied trades which went to make the community self sufficient. The abbey was the 'big house', and all that took place within its walls or on its farmland became guidance or gossip for the local people.

The food for the college was provided by the abbey, and the huge brown and white loaves from the bakery had a fresh, crusty and wholesome flavour, mouth watering even in memory. 'Brown bread! Brown bread' became the rallying call of the rugby team.

This monastic and scholastic centre was rich in the talent and personalities of its lay and clerical staff. The most endearing and outstanding character was the president, Father Ailbe Sadlier; but nobody ever called him that. I will always remember 'The Boss' as an oil painting. The Cistercian habit fitted him well; he was tall and of moderate build put protruding slightly at the stomach. His sparse hair was pure white. He presided firmly but benevolently over his family of 220 boys. He supervised them at prayer and in the refectory, corresponded with their parents, worried when they were ill, and hooshed them on with a belt of a hurley on the backside when they slowed down going through a doorway.

In keeping with such a character there were the poses — all memorable; arms akimbo, feet apart, and chin pushed out, he would fumble for words which would not come because of mounting rage at some rowdy display. Stern faced, with his head bent in confessional concentration, he listened to a small boy ask for an early sleep which would excuse him evening study. Again the hands were on his hips and his feet wide spread, but this time his face was cast upwards and his teeth working as his interest was captivated by a companion's talk. Or hurley in hand at the sideline, his frame fully stretched and arching forward, he would place his hand over his eyes, and pucker his brow in many ridges as he peered intently towards the scrum. I have quite forgotten which pose he held when I told him at the age of eleven that I wanted to be a Canadian mounted policeman.

We were at Roscrea six years, we studied for exams, struggled for places on the rugby and hurling teams, sang in the operettas, suffered the bullies and suddenly found ourselves seniors. Before we realized what had happened we were young men sitting our final exams. Secondary school ended for me in June 1939, and by the time of our second college reunion in the autumn of 1940, some of my classmates had already died in the war.

The sweet days of youth were nearly past and we

left Roscrea forever to make our way through a world in turmoil. The choice of a career led me to an engineering school in a Dublin university, but by the time of my first examination in June of 1940, I was in the army.

At the university however some of the aviation seeds which had been dormant in my mind for years had slowly started to germinate. In the rural community from which I came aviation and all that went with it was significantly remote. Few aeroplanes crossed the skies of Mayo and magazines and models were not easy to come by. Nevertheless, there were three aeroplanes that I always treasured in my child's mind. The biggest of these I had only heard about. It was the Vickers Vimy biplane that Alcock and Brown had flown across the Atlantic. They landed in a bog in the nearby county of Galway. However I had actually seen two aeroplanes.

The first was an army biplane which had crashed in the townland of Knockmore. I watched with awe as the military brought it away like a crushed butterfly, with crumpled wings in one trailer and battered body in another.

The second was a more practical experience.

Never shall I forget the day that a boyhood companion rushed into our house and said: 'Quick quick, there's an aeroplane landed in a field at Pontoon.' We adopted as our own this high wing monoplane, never deigning to touch it but posing for numerous photographs beside the propeller or underneath the wings We sat for hours in the summer grass admiring the sleek lines and making endless speculations on the functions of all its moving parts. Each day after school we would pedal full tilt along the four dusty miles to Pontoon until, one morning, a strange noise filled the classroom, and died away. With it went my dream; our aeroplane had gone.

The physical idea of becoming a pilot had never

really entered my mind, primarily because it was an unusual enough occupation to be out of reach of even the fantasies of small boys in the west of Ireland.

Collinstown in County Dublin had been an RAF airfield which was completed at the time of the first World War, and during the late 30s an uncle of mine was employed there. I made many visits to the place with him to see its reconstruction, and to watch the comings and goings of commercial aeroplanes. This is now Dublin Airport.

The periphery of the landing field was picked out with white and red boundary markers placed at close intervals around the fencing, illumination at night was provided by four large lights; three had static beams, but the fourth could be aimed in any direction by a remote switching unit in the control tower. Unlike today, aeroplanes then did not carry powerful generators and lights. There was a blind landing system which was an unusual installation for that time, an illuminated wind direction indicator, and a full meteorological observatory with a staff of forecasters.

In later years I flew as co-pilot to Captain Ivan B. Hammond in one of Aer Lingus' first aeroplanes. It was not an easy machine to handle on the ground, but 'Hammy' had his own particular method which allowed the aeroplane no opportunity to swing on take-off. With four throttles at immediate full power we used to lurch and bump across the airfield, until finally the little aeroplane had enough speed to fly. The whole business was accomplished to 'Hammy's' version of 'The Mountains of Mourne'.

He was master at nosing his way in and out of any place on radio bearings. Much later that day when we returned to Dublin, he would glide down to the west to lose height and turn back after two minutes to glue us on to the inbound bearing. If the clouds were low 'Hammy' would push the side window back and stick his bald head out into the streaming mist to peer for the boundary fence. When a red and white marker loomed up we knew we were there. As it disappeared beneath the cockpit window, he closed the throttles, and we sank softly into the damp grass from the darkness of the winter's evening.

III

In December of 1939 the Department of Defence advertised in the daily newspapers for candidates for short service commissions in the Irish Army Air Corps. I wrote immediately in reply, and with a large group of young Irishmen, was called for an interview to St. Bricin's Military Hospital.

The army doctors examined us from end to end and inevitably our numbers dwindled. I remember one big fellow from Galway whose urine was not of the required quality roaring at the rest of us as he stumbled out the door: 'To think I came the whole bloody way from Ballinasloe to pee into a feckin jar!' Others of us were more forunate and, passing the medical, were interviewed by an army board. When it came to my turn I walked in with all the aplomb of youth and sat before a stern row of officers of various ranks and corps, all immaculately attired in high-collared, full-buttoned tunics. I found no difficulty in answering their questions. Finally a young officer wearing a pair of gold embroidered wings addressed me in Irish and I replied with some hesitancy: we talked about salmon fishing in Mayo.

I got off the bus at Baldonnel Cross on a fine afternoon on 7 May, 1940, accompanied by a young man from the North of Ireland. Walking up the road we saw small aeroplanes wheeling in the sky like lazy birds; they were circling the airfield at the military aviation centre of Baldonnel. By late evening 21 cadets of that class of 1940 were assembled.

The group consists of a range of men from old school tie to ex-soldier; some evolved a drill all their own and others had no interest whatever in basic infantry training. 'When do we fly?' was the perpetual query; but the army ignored the gripes and educated the class to basic infantry standard. We were divided into two sections and trained in all the elementary subjects that made a military pilot. One unit flew in the morning while the other was on the ground; we changed duties in the afternoon. Mysteries of engines and airframes, military law and discipline, infantry training and machine gun design, navigation, airman-ship and airlaw, all followed each other in stimulating sequence.

Though it was years ago, the instructors who gave of their best to that class of 1940 are even now walking in front of my pen, tumbling out of the years with all their idiosyncrasies and human failings. One dear, fat, middle-aged sergeant was the daddy of them all; he never had a penny or a stitch of civvy clothes but he loved his ball of malt and his class of cadets. I can see him now on a hot day in August: cap tilted back, tunic open, and colourful basketball singlet bared to the sun; he rested on his backside in the grass and taunted us about cold pints of beer as our leggings worked their way up the calves of our sweaty legs. Our introduction to this wonderful character was through his reputation of having had the throttle of a Bristol Fighter disappeared up his arse when the aircraft flew into Bray Head.

Barrack life for army cadets was similar to that of its soldiers. Lights went out on the sound of the bugle and there was no snuggling deeper into the grey woollen blankets when reveille sounded in the morning. Our sleep was broken by the crash of the billet door and the drill sergeant shouting: 'Rise and feckin' shine, ye may be officers tomorrow for all I care but this place is like a bloody pig-sty!' After the initial shock he would become more formal: 'Cadet Quigley, get your arse out of them feckin' blankets.'

Friday was a night of exceptional activity, since on Saturday morning a full inspection of billets, kit and personnel was carried out in every army post. A dirty rifle barrel or a badly kept kit usually meant the loss of a weekend pass.

First Lieutenant Mossie Quinlan, my flying instructor, was stout but goodlooking, with a small moustache and a drawl that partly masked his Kerry accent. We went to fly in a helmet and goggles, leather gloves, fur-lined boots, and a teddy bear flying suit. With the lot bottomed off by a parachute, I ambled beside Mossie to the aeroplane.

'O.K., Quigs, you start it up,' he drawled into the speaking tubes, 'and I'll give you the procedure as we go along.'

I shouted to the corporal at the engine: 'Switches off, fuel on, throttles closed, suck in!' The man repeated the order and tugged the propeller around by hand to draw the fuel into the cylinders.

On his shout of 'Contact!' I switched on the ignition, repeated his call, and a final heave of the propeller started the engine.

Mossie taxied it out for take-off, zig-zagging across the grass until eventually he lined up near the wind sock and opened up the power. We got off the ground fairly rapidly, and as the aeroplane climbed he gave me ten minutes of scenic flying with a supplementary patter, while, stomach turning, I stared in disbelief at the postage stamp fields. Then it happened, as I had feared: I started to feel sick. Mossie, kind man that he was, put us down near the pill box in the centre of the 'drome. It became routine, 'I'll taxi down the hill a bit where the chaps won't see you, Quigs.' There I would get out and bring up my entire breakfast or lunch, depending on which detail we were on. I persevered, and although I frequently felt sick in the air, I kept it grimly down. In six weeks the problem had disappeared.

We flew almost every day and in the evenings compared notes on our progress. With some it was not going so well, and before we received our wings the following year, five were washed out for various reasons.

The plane we flew, the Magister, was a robust little monoplane constructed entirely from laminated impregnated plywood. It was easy to fly and fitted with simple flaps; these are aerodynamic devices which allow an aeroplane to be flown at a slower speed when approaching to land. The cockpits were in tandem with the instructor occupying the front, and communicating through a speaking tube. Throttles and flight controls were interconnected, which meant that teacher and pupil were in continuous contact. One day an instructor disconnected the front control column and waved it in the air to give his pupil confidence — not to be outdone the trainee removed his and waved it back!

Mossie Quinlan was a good teacher, and he tolerantly introduced me to straight and level flying, takeoffs and landings, and everything that was simple and right way up. Soon the exercises went into looping and rolling. The chimney of the paper mill at Clondalkin was our favourite aiming point, and with the comforting sight of Mossie's big helmet stolidly in front of me, I would ease the nose of the Magister down on that target, listening to Mossie's patter through the earphones: 'Ease her down a little more — O.K. that's fast enough — up slowly now, keep easing the stick back.' The little aeroplane would climb up into the blue until land and sky changed places, and we were over the top of the loop. Eventually the art was perfected, and our favourite chimney came floating back into view in the correct position.

Each instructor followed the same pattern. As his pupil pilot became more adept he would quietly and unexpectedly ease the throttle back and allow the student to select a field and glide safely towards it, only to have him shy away again when he was satisfied that a successful forced landing could have been made.

Next we progressed to spinning and recovery. Up went the nose with the power off, and as the speed died, the noise of the rushing air grew less and was punctuated by grunts from the throttled engine. With the momentum dissipated, Mossie would pull the stick all the way back and apply full right rudder. The nose would lurch down to the right, and the fields and the canal to the west of Baldonnel would start to rotate. It was no doubt a kaleidoscopic spectacle for those who could appreciate it; I got sick.

Finally, one of the biggest moments in my flying career arrived. We taxied to the take-off position and the instructor clambered out of the cockpit; I realised he was sending me solo. I lined up on a point to keep it straight as I had been taught, but all the while I was acutely conscious of the empty cockpit in front of me. I got the plane off the ground with surprising ease, and was around the circuit and lining up for a landing before I knew what I had done. We arrived in a series of bounces, but I had performed them unaided with only eight and a half hours of flight instruction.

After the first solo, the tuition progressed into more complex manoeuvres which proved too difficult for some of the class. Fortunately, there were no fatalities, although there were two crashes, the most memorable of which occurred when a tiny plane suddenly arrived in the midst of the wheelbarrows and shovels of a work party building a pillbox.

We entered the realm of slow and flick rolls, stall turns, and inverted flying, until each exercise was perfected and checked out by an instructor. No cargo of stout on its way by canal barge from Dublin to Limerick was safe from the embryo fighter pilots; we straffed them endlessly.

I think night flying was the most fascinating experience of all. The flare path (a line of lights indicating the runway) was marked out by paraffin flares positioned along the grass. There was a landing light at the beginning of the path to give illumination — the ambulance was parked beside it. Other units were exercising and we watched reconnaissance and army co-operation planes going in and out on the landing strip. Unless we were extremely careful it was very easy to land over or on top of another aircraft; somebody did one night, but got away with it.

My first night flight was a typical one. Lumbering the Magister to the line up point, we acknowledged the steady green which was flashed from the control van; this authorised us to go. The take-off proved to be relatively easy, and although the light was poor, the feel of the aeroplane was enough, and we were away with a lurch into the darkness. Flying around in a wide circuit, I watched the spectacle below. The barrack lights at Baldonnel shone faintly, but the open doors of the hangars spilt their illumination brightly on the aprons in front. The city lights were clear until a large drifting patch of cloud switched them out area by area and left beneath only a faint grey amorphous glow. The flare path at Baldonnel appeared as only a small glimmering pencil in the midst of great darkness. The instructor explained that when close in on final, the angle of glide indicators would come clearly into view and help us with our approach. They loomed up amber and green and I throttled back slowly. We settled down with flaps out and speed reduced; both the lights were now green and we adjusted our glide to remain at the correct angle. The little wooden aeroplane flew out of the night with a rush into the lighted area of the strip, and bumped across the grass to a stop.

Next we flew the Avro Cadet, a fabric covered biplane. It was slower than the Magister, and required more skill in aerobatics to achieve as perfect a manoeuvre. I can still hear and feel the swish of the sideslip as it see-sawed from side to side to lose height on the approach. The instrument panel was primitive. Though I had 47 hours flying time, it took about 20 minutes in that Avro, and one not very large patch of stratus cloud, to demonstrate my limitations in elementary flying. I became disoriented and flew around in circles in the cloud, not possessing enough skill to fly up and out of it, and not having enough daring to risk flying down through it. Eventually at a low height the cloud rejected us; and steeples, chimneys, trees, buses, and people slipped underneath as we drifted by in bewilderment and confusion. Fortunately I found a small open area where the demon would fit and, with a few tail swishes to lose height, I put it down in the cow patch and rang Baldonnel for help.

*   *   *

Landing ground, airstrip, airfield, airport, aerodrome; these are all words with the same broad meaning; a place frequented by aeroplanes. Somehow the name 'aerodrome' captures the magic, giving an image of a large open place in the countryside where 'heavier than air' machines are flown, and onlookers mesmerised by the variety of paraphernalia.

An aerodrome was a fascinating place; full of exciting mechanical activity and yet so woefully at the mercy of weather. There were old lattice timbered hangars, runways cut in the grass, wind socks and a water tower, an armoury store and a fire tender, and wafting across the tarmac the whiff of high octane exhaust gas.

Not yet had the sophisticated whine of jet engines and the profusion of multicoloured lights and signs reached even our imaginations. Paint in if you will a vintage biplane fighter at full throttle on the blocks, a sergeant in the cockpit with his hair streaming from the propeller's rush, and two of his men spread-eagled on either side holding the tailplane down. Search for the sound and the smell as the Rolls Royce engine bellows blue smoke from the exhausts. Watch the tail unit writhe and vibrate in the slipstream as the overalls of its occupants press into their bodies and grotesquely outline their shape. If now your canvas is complete, and you have smelt the exhaust fumes, let us have the sergeant switch the engine off; since even to your unpractised and unfamiliar ear the work of his fitters has not been in vain.

Gormanston in County Meath was a typical aerodrome. No concrete runway seared its virgin grass. It is close by the sea, and many times the near stillness of the dusk and the soft swish of the wavelets were stabbed by the distant rapid crack of some turret gunner testing his guns on the way to Germany. Further up along the coast from Gormanston was the big railway bridge across the Boyne at Drogheda, guarded day and night.

One early morning, a sentry stood on the long span shrouded in his greatcoat against the river breeze: the water was 100 feet down in the gloom below. Two RAF Spitfires, expertly camouflaged and low on the river, came straight at him, the wicked disc of their propeller arcs pinning him to the parapet. One fighter continued low, and went under the bridge like an express train entering a tunnel; the other pulled up slightly to go over the top of the arched span. It's slipstream blew acrid exhaust smoke into the motionless face of the sentry.

The echo of the two Merlin engines was still reverberating around the waking town when he got to his telephone and called the guard room. The sergeant listened patiently, and replied: 'Arra, shur all them flying fellas is mad, Mickey; the same thing happened yesterday morning, only they were German Messerschmitts!!'

* * *

Captain Bartley O'Connor will confirm the date; I am almost certain it was the night of 22 October 1967. Bartley has been a friend of mine for 25 years, and I know that he is psychic. A frail old lady frequently used to appear in his house. Her ghostly transparency terrified his dog and scared gaping messenger boys who viewed the spectre over Bartley's shoulder when he opened the hall door. None of the family made any attempt to communicate with the woman; she came and went at varying hours of the day and night. I had no encounter with this spirit. My own experience of the supernatural was limited to a mild but active poltergeist who haunted a block of flats in which I spent my early married life. He swung the pictures on the wall, creaked phantom footsteps on the stairs and finally flaunted his impish talents by splitting our two cut glass ashtrays.

Whether these experiences have anything to do with the events of the night — I will leave up to you.

On 22 October 1967, I was taking a flight out of Chicago to Dublin. There was a shortage of first officers, so O'Connor and I were crewing the aeroplane as captain and co-pilot, alternating on the duties.

It was a beautiful night and we flew serenely along at 37,000 feet with stars and gentle thoughts for company. The senior hostess came into the cockpit and said: 'Captain, we are two dinners short. I have two passengers in row four who were not there when we left. They're not listed on the seating form, and I think there's something very unusual about them!'

Bartley said nothing but I got out of the seat, put on my cap and jacket and went back to the cabin. My initial concern was that there was now insufficient food on board; we had 122 passengers and the flight kitchen had provided meals for only 120. The problem was later solved by making up two extra trays with some food filched from the crew catering. Nevertheless it seemed strange to me that these two people were not listed on the passenger manifest, so I presented myself to them and explained my problem. He in turn introduced both himself and the woman in a foreign accent with an inflection totally strange to my ear.

'My name is Vaalkar and this is my wife — my sincere apologies to you, Captain, if you were concerned about our presence, but we joined the flight at a late stage.'

He continued to talk to me in a precise tone, each word perfectly pronounced, each sentence beautifully phrased. Our flow of conversation was colloquial and ranged over politics and world affairs, but when he questioned me about the aeroplane the query was straight to the point. The man gave the impression that he was filing the answers as if they were being fed to a computer. 'Of what metal is this vessel composed? Why relate your speed to that of sound? Are you limited to this method of space travel? Are you confined to jet thrust for propulsive force?'

His wife, who had remained silent, spoke now in a similar metallic voice: 'Sergi, you must not question so. What will this man think of our manners?' This was my cue and I made a polite excuse and walked back to the cockpit.

'What was that all about?' said Bartley. 'You were a long time. Was she a good looking bird?'

I made no reply but sat into the co-pilot seat, fastened the safety belt slowly, and stared ahead in silence. This time it was O'Connor's turn to look across at me. He jabbed me with his elbow and said: 'Give!' He still remembers clearly what I said to him: 'Just go back in a few minutes and have a peep at that couple in row four — no, I'm not going to tell you anything else — just go back.'

I continued to look out ahead into the night and waited. Twenty minutes went by and I passed our 'forty West' position to Gander. It took me nearly as long to transmit it since static interference was heavy and the frequencies on both radio sets were plagued by a faint background whistle. Communication was bad all night, possibly due to the unusually active Aurora Borealis — the Northern Lights. However, there must have been another disturbance as well, for some moments later the navigator said: 'I have been monitoring the radar scope since I picked up the weather ship and there has been a continuous interference trace. The last time I saw that signal was during the war.'

Bartley O'Connor came back into the cockpit.

'Well?' I asked.

'I don't quite know what to think. Did you notice their skin?'

'Not particularly. The lights in that area are low.'

'Well,' he said, 'It has the most unusual texture. Both of those characters have the smoothest, whitest skin; no pores, no blemishes, no creases. I am absolutely sure of that because the woman dropped a book and I picked it up for her. In fact we all picked it up together, and their hands were directly beside mine.'

'So?' I said, 'they might have been Egyptians or high caste Indians.'

'That's possible,' Bartley replied, 'but did you study their clothes? The tailoring was perfect. It was a strange material, and cut angularly; no curves at all, even on

29

the bird. The whole set up reminded me of a tailor's dummy.' He told me the woman spoke to him for some time and asked the most peculiar questions, showing herself a person of unusual intelligence.

I lost interest in the incident as we flew across the lonely ocean. O'Connor reverted his gaze to the side window and drew me over to look at the Northern Lights. There was an arc of white intensity stretching along the polar horizon. The light was changing in colour within itself like a reflection in the heavens from a vast amphitheatre; search lights within the core were impatiently sweeping through the brilliance. The display was endless and if one glanced away for a few seconds, and then looked back, he could see that a myriad of changes was taking place within that apparently symmetrical pattern. Apart from the splendour, there was something very unusual going on but even Bartley could not be sure as to what it precisely was, although he had been watching for two and a half hours.

We flew on into the dawn with the curtains closed and the cabin lights switched off. All our passengers slumbered, including the couple in row four. 'Thirty West' the positions went by until at 'Fifteen West' the night was over, and we had caught up with the sun. Its rays focused on the temperature sensor in the corner of the cockpit, and the false signal chilled the air.

'How are our friends in row four?' I asked.

'They're not in their seats now,' Bernice replied. 'I presume they've gone to the washrooms.'

They were not in the washrooms, nor indeed in the aeroplane. The Northern Lights were gone and with them the sweeping searchlights and the strangeness which Bartley had seen in the night sky. We went back separately to where they had been sitting. There was an extraordinary exotic odour about their seats, and the white linen headrests were now flecked with a fine deposit of graphite.

'They'll never believe us,' said Captain Bartley O'Connor. They never did.

I dismissed the whole business from my mind, only recalling it a short time ago when the Russians released a news bulletin on their cosmonaut Valkaar, whom they had been unable to recover from a polar orbit.

IV

In common with all aspects of man's endeavour, certain fundamental factors apply to the role of the pilot: man is fallible, of varying temperament, and subject to fear, nervousness, and anxiety. There exists also the shadows that come and go from domestic problems, human relations, food, sleep and health; these things affect the man and his performance can be diminished or enhanced accordingly. Pilot selection techniques and subsequent training provide a band of performance within which the individual must be able to operate, and he enters that band knowing that the system will ignore his personal affairs or feelings unless they should surface to destroy his norm.

This is not to say that authority ignores the mental and physical health of an airman; on the contrary the medical standards are high and constantly monitored. Phased training and practical experience ensure that, although a man's reactions may be slowed or his judgements impaired by emotion, his response will normally fall within the safe band of acceptable action and decision. Human error does occur, but its consequences are limited where there is a cockpit atmosphere of technical competence and harmony. The minimum pilot crew for a large commercial passenger aeroplane is two, most carry three, hence there is a multiple assessment of any decision or action taken.

A modern airline now provides its own pilots. In the past, fully trained and experienced men were available from the military or from private flying schools. The Irish airline, Aer Lingus originally used these methods of recruitment, but in latter years the company has found it necessary to set up a training scheme of its own. Up to now 100 young Irishmen have been selected and instructed in this system, and are currently employed by Aer Lingus. The tuition is mainly paid for by the airline, but the student bears a proportion of the cost through deduction from his monthly salary during the first years of his employment.

The selection processes serve to thin down the large number of men who apply. Intelligence test patterns common in business and industry are used to rate the candidate. He is also checked for mechanical aptitude, so necessary to enable him to absorb subsequently all the technicalities involved in the career. Psychology tests are completed in consultation with a university.

The talents of the individual are finally screened by a board of executive pilots and flying instructors. The panel carries out lengthy interviews and considers the reports from previous sessions; then it makes the final choices. The plan was originally to train all these young men in a school provided by the Irish Army Air Corps, but the facilities there could not cater for such a large number, and therefore a considerable proportion of the total to date have been trained in England.

The screening process may seem overly cautious but it is essential to pick men who show aptitude for the job, and who adapt readily to a novel environment and to other crew members, with whom they will work in close proximity for long hours. There is no attempt to seek out genius or social status amongst those who apply. The programme has been devised to select average young Irishmen who have passed through the secondary school system, and who have some mechanical aptitude and knowledge.

The training and curriculum for the students differs very little from that of their military counterparts in the initial stages; this early training takes just a year and generally the failure rate is low. The civil pilot finally graduates with an Instrument Rating and a Commercial Licence. To obtain such a rating the trainee is required to demonstrate his competence to a government inspector by operating an aeroplane on the airways. A Commercial Licence entitles the holder to fly as a co-pilot on commercial aircraft.

To reach higher qualification he returns to the airline for further flying and ground school: here he is brought up to the standard required for the operation of large commercial aeroplanes on world wide routes. This phase takes six months and during that time the cadet undergoes government examinations which will licence him for the operation of this new aircraft type. These are written tests covering the technical and operating aspect of the new equipment.

During the initial stages, and later during the career of the pilot, the simulator has a most important function. This equipment is an inseparable part of a modern airline, and is expensive in capital cost and up-keep. The simulator is a faithful reproduction of the cockpit of an aeroplane. Its switches, flying controls and levers, all perform precisely the same function as they do in reality. The instruments are genuine, and give height, speed, direction and position information to the pilot, and react correspondingly to his inputs. Further realism is imparted by movement of the trainer in response to the controls.

The instructor has an electronic panel from which he can feed any given emergency situation into the machine. Later models have computers where it is only necessary to programme the selected faults and they trigger themselves off at the required time, leaving the pilot to cope with engine failures, electrical difficulties, control faults, in any desired combination. All the basics of pilot proficiency and safety are practiced and perfected in such surroundings.

My airline has always named its aeroplanes after saints, so appropriately enough our simulators are called 'Saint Thetic.'

Aircrew and ground engineers go 'back to school' two or three times a year, for refresher courses or to absorb new information. Legislation requires that a pilot's competence and reaction to emergencies are checked twice a year by an instructor. Practice emergency evacuation drills take place regularly, and a complete medical examination is carried out every six months by state doctors before the licence is renewed.

I first gave a sample in St. Bricin's Military Hospital of Dublin 1940, and ever since I visit in December and June; a total of about 400 civil and military pilots and navigators are examined there twice during the year. The first call is to the laboratory for a specimen. The urine can have no sugar under test or the donor is in trouble: it is difficult to resist the temptation of dropping a lump of sugar into the beaker of somebody you do not like, as specimens of all the colonels, captains, and co-pilots lie in neatly labelled jars on the table. It is a short distance to the X-Ray theatre where the chest is expanded on the command 'Breathe in deeply now, and hold it.' The machine has a butt plate which goes right up under the chin and we stood at attention, chest out, feeling as if we were ready for the guillotine.

The eyes are checked for clarity, width and depth of sight, muscle balance, correction, and colour blindness. Finally the doctor peers into those windows of your soul with an opthalmascope; but he is only looking at the optic nerve, and not at your works and pumps.

Next is the cardiograph: an instrument which records movements of the heart. You lie on a couch with wires taped to wrists and ankles, and a nurse moves the terminals around the heart. It is best to relax, and think of cosmonauts and astronauts, and consider yourself lucky; at least you are not weightless. Since the shirt is off the moment is now convenient for the general physical. Here the doctor checks the blood pressure, heart, pulse rate before and after exercise, weight, hands for undue tremor, and muscle for nerve response. Now you adopt a pose like the boxer John L. Sullivan — left arm outstretched with fingers clenched, and the head turned sharply away to the right — the face is grimacing because you know the time has come for the blood sample needle to be inserted in the blue vein standing proud in the centre of that tensed left arm.

When the ear, nose, and throat man has satisfied himself as to the condition of these organs, the airman enters a soundproof cabinet; he sits on a chair and places a headset over his ears. Looking at the nurse through the window from that noise proof refuge there is a choice of environmental feelings: being in a diving bell, a confessional, a gas chamber, a goldfish bowl, a Turkish bath, or a fortune teller's booth. The reverie is ended by the consciousness of a dull note in the left ear which has been induced by controls on an audio machine, a button must be pushed in response when the sound is first heard. The nurse marks this point on a graded sheet and adjusts the acoustic unit to give a note of higher tone; and so on, the pitch increasing until, at 50 years and having listened to pistons and turbines for 32 of them, the higher frequencies escape me.

I always stop for a pint on the way home — a combination of thirst and relief.

High standards in the maintenance of an aeroplane are essential in order to reduce accident risk. Manufacturers carry out exhaustive tests on airframes, engines, instruments, and equipment; many of the items are tested to destruction by mechanical jigs which simulate stresses and strains far in excess of those usually encountered. From these experiments the expected life of a component is deduced, and thus an inspection or replacement programme is devised with ample margin to spare. An airline usually imposes even more demanding inspection requirements, and is itself obliged to carry out this work under government legislation and surveillance.

One system used in airline practice involves a planned progressive inspection of the entire aircraft. The final stage of this process is the removal of the engines and dismemberment of the airframe itself into wings, tail, and rudder, for examination. All of these steps might suggest a frenzy of opening and closing of mechanical parts to check their condition; this is not the case since undue and unnecessary tampering with mechanical, electrical or hydraulic equipment will usually tend to induce failures.

The service routine which accompanies an aeroplane after it lands in the enroute phase of its day is uncomplicated. Ground engineers attend to its needs of fuel, oil, hydraulic fluid, and water. The pilot or flight engineer inspects the exterior, paying particular attention to the undercarriage and tyre condition. He searches carefully for any sign of damage to the fuselage skin. He checks for fluid leaks and security of panels; he ensures that all fixed and movable control surfaces are in acceptable condition. Maintenance or repair is carried out if something is not in proper working order.

Within the cockpit, the checks are more detailed and are tailored to each phase of flight; the pilot must know what he is looking for in each test, but the physical act of performing it is spelt out clearly and chronologically on his check list. So, too, with emergency equipment and unusual situations; each drill is the result of technical experiment and practical experience, and most of the actions are relatively simple: those that are not are elaborated to avoid confusion. The drills and procedures are backed up by a quick reference, easy-to-read, technical library carried in the cockpit.

Besides the quality control that the authority maintains it also requires that performance be surveyed, and in consequence each aeroplane is withdrawn periodically from service, and its flight and engine behaviour checked and recorded. It was for this purpose that we flew a DC3 out one hazy afternoon; I shut down an engine and feathered the propellor at the appropriate time and climbed exactly at the specified speed. Two engineers meticulously annotated their observation sheets and logged the climb performance. We were doing very well until it came to the stall tests. 'Ease her back,' said Tug. 'With the power off, allow the speed to decay at one knot a second until we reach the stall.' It was my first full performance test and I was doing it carefully.

Seventy knots, 69, 67, 66 and still no stall: it was obvious to everybody but me that I was going into it too slowly. We hung there in the haze of that afternoon, the nose going higher and higher, until in desperation, the plane dropped a wing and fell over on its back. I gently eased it out of the ensuing dive, repeated the manoeuvre correctly, and returned to land. The ground engineer slammed into the cockpit and yelled: 'What the hell were you fellas doing; there's shit all over the ceiling.' So there was; nobody had emptied the honey bucket at the rear of the cabin and our last desperate lurch has thrown its contents along the ceiling.

An elderly aunt of mine used to say that the sky was only for birds, and certainly some of man's early attempts to fly were ornithological in the extreme; but flapping canvas wings were replaced in time by rugged structures, an internal combustion engine, metal propellers and jet propulsion. Man, in his own slow clumsy way, developed sophisticated control systems to imitate the movements that belonged from birth to the smallest insect in the sky. My aunt was correct to some degree, as man cannot fly without his machine, but thousands of airmen have finally brought the designer's efforts to fruition in the safe operation of large and speedy commercial aircraft.

There are those that think that modern aircraft are too big or too fast. I met a man a short time ago who mourned the old DC3; perhaps this is because passengers felt more at ease when they were in closer touch with the flight crew. Whilst flying aeroplanes of small capacity, like DC3, it took a long time to fly a short distance and pilots were in closer communion with those in the cabin. In my early years, there was a type of passenger who was dedicated and who flew both for exhilaration and necessity. He enjoyed the novelty of a diversion to another airfield and was classified as a 'regular.' There was little fear in the make up of this particular traveller, but there were many who felt doubt and anxiety, and who flew only because they had to. Others tranquilized their fears with alcohol or sedatives, but the bulk accepted it for what it was: a safe convenient method of travel.

To-day the aeroplane is moving so fast, that the journey is over before most of the occupants realise it; on long distance flights they settle down to the comforts provided, and relax in surroundings so like a hotel that they forget whatever qualms they had when they boarded. We are becoming blasé about aviation as it becomes more common and more necessary. One cannot, without gross inconvenience, travel from one country to the other without flying.

Some of us are afraid of the unknown and of the 'risk' involved in aviation; perhaps here the reader will find a panacea to allay such trepidation. The aeroplane is a very safe vehicle in the hands of trained pilots; its structure is strong, its engines dependable, and the chances of something drastic happening when flying are considerably less than they are when crossing the street. As an airline pilot I would recommend that you get up there and fly! Leave the worrying to the Lord, and the statistics to me.

V

'Mike, tell New York Control that we're declaring an emergency, and ask for an immediate priority clearance to land on arrival at Kennedy.'

'O.K. Skipper,' he drawled back at me, and then added, 'and while I'm at it, what time would you like me to tell him to expect us?'

We were both clearly aware of the precise details of the situation!

Four tons of fuel remained on our Boeing 720 jet.

The altitude was 15,000 feet — an undesirable but unalterable height.

The minimum possible fuel consumption was four tons per hour.

The main radio entry beacon serving the New York area was Riverhead, and on the distance measuring equipment it was 180 nautical miles. Kennedy Airport at New York was a further 40 miles.

Severe headwinds had brought our speed down to 180 nautical miles per hour.

All airports within range were closed by snow storms except Kennedy. Mike had earlier said to me that the only possible way we could reach it was by rowing the last 50 miles up Long Island Sound with empty tanks.

One hundred and ten passengers were on board with no knowledge of any problem.

The flight was bound from Shannon to Boston, Massachusetts.

I turned to the navigator and said 'I think we'll have a cup of coffee, Brendan. How about you?'

'Make it three, Skipper,' he replied, and then added very quietly, 'Where do you come from, Aidan?'

'Foxford, County Mayo,' I answered.

I pressed the cabin call and the senior hostess entered the cockpit.

'Three coffees, Joan, please.'

'Sugar and milk for all, Captain?'

'Yes,' I replied, 'and by the way we are diverting to New York. Boston is out with snow. I'll make an announcement to the passengers after the coffee.'

'How much longer have we then?' she enquired.

'One hour — perhaps more,' I said slowly.

I had been short on fuel before, and to overcome the problem all the factors which the elements had introduced had to be rationalised, so that sound judgement and practical measures were brought to bear to solve the difficulty. This time it was different; we still had all the factors, but there was no solution.

Pre-flight planning procedures for the operation of a long distance jet are comprehensive, yet when the aeroplane is in its natural environment tailwinds often change to headwinds, temperatures tend to be higher than expected and airport forecasts may be overly optimistic; sometimes, too, planned cruising heights are not available because of other traffic. All of this usually compounds into a single problem: fuel reserves dwindle below what is planned. To counter such difficulties, the pilot is trained by experience and technical background to apply his judgement and, if necessary, to alter his flight pattern by an enroute diversion, a speed or height change, a reappraisal of fuel reserves, or, ultimately, a selection of an alternate airport for the final landing.

The global atmosphere is constantly being examined by scientists who identify temperatures and pressures, clouds, wind direction and humidities. Their results are conveyed by teleprinters to a world-wide network of meteorological offices. It is from such information, combined with aeroplane performance data and fuel consumption tables, that a selected route is planned to provide minimum flight time and maximum fuel economy. Contingency reserves are added for possible diversion to alternate landing places.

The dispatcher had prepared a route plan for our flight from a survey of the weather charts plotted at 0600 hours. At the briefing, he explained to my crew that Boston weather was forecast good, with Windsor Locks in Connecticut as alternate, and Gander in Newfoundland as an enroute emergency stop. Subsequent events had proved the meteorological forecasts incorrect, but despite a constant weather monitor all along the flight this fact remained undisclosed until it was too late.

One hundred miles from Boston was the original planned starting point of descent.

The Boston weather was a broadcast recording — the repetitive voice in our loudspeaker said: 'Boston weather information: Boston sky obscured at 1500 feet, visibility three and a half miles, wind velocity Northeast at four miles per hour.' The message clicked off and then repeated again.

'Windsor Locks weather okay as well?' I asked the co-pilot.

'Okay Skipper,' he replied, 'and so is New York.'

'Fuel?' I nodded towards the third pilot.

'Alternate diversion fuel, plus a ton: seven tons total.'

I eased the four throttles back and the Boeing sank down gently into the night; but at 12,000 feet, and 40 miles from Boston, the flight dispatcher at New York called us urgently: 'Boston is out with a heavy snowstorm, wind gusting to 45 knots, visibility down to quarter mile in snow.'

'Standby, I will call you back,' I replied.

We climbed up to 15,000 feet and decided it was the best altitude.

'How much now?' I asked the third pilot.

'Four tons, Captain,' came the reply, and I realised there was nowhere to go.

I had visualised this moment many times, and been apprehensive as to what my reactions would be; but my mood now was cold, calculating, and emotionally relaxed, and I sensed that the other three felt the same.

'Do you know of any military airfields along here, Skipper?' the navigator asked.

'I do,' I said, 'but the weather is the same in this area, and their set up is completely different from ours. If we made an approach things could become worse than they are now.' We flew on through the night, the soft grey cloud beneath now stretching to nowhere.

'I have another weather report, Captain, from Windsor Locks! Four hundred feet and a half mile in snow; they've just opened.'

'Thanks, Mike,' I said to the co-pilot. 'Get a radar clearance direct to Windsor Locks.'

We went down through the grey carpet, turning to the radar controller's instructions. He locked us on to the runway landing aid at a distance of ten miles. The cloud started to break at 500 feet, and I stole an anxious glance away from the instrument panel and out into the lighted snow flakes; a friendly hand pushed my head back down. Moments later the wheels mushed gently into the soft runway snow. We had made it with only enough fuel left for another 20 minutes.

Man is fallible, and this is undoubtedly a factor in some air crashes. Machines can not be perfect: the computer is only as good as the programme with which it was fed. Mechanical devices can break down, elect-

42

rical power failures do occur, structures collapse, and men die; these are things that blight all endeavour in work or leisure. So, too, with aviation; it extracts its toll as the price of progress, but at a considerably lower rate than does road transport.

I have no intention of manipulating statistics to produce favourable results: it is best that the reader assesses the facts for himself. However, since statistics in themselves are presented in many different forms, it is sometimes difficult to find a clear parallel so that a comparison can be made with other means of transport. I have availed of data produced by the International Civil Aviation Organisation; a group composed of most of the nations of the world. In the accident survey for 1969, the study stated that it is unquestionable that present day jet traffic is considerably safer than was the earlier traffic by propeller aircraft on the same network; the higher percentage of the accidents were to propeller aircraft even though most of the passenger miles were flown by jets. In 1969 a total of 1,295 passengers were killed in crashes of commercial aviation aircraft on world wide operation. In that same time 348 million people were carried on scheduled aircraft services alone (regular airlines). In Ireland during that period 462 persons were killed on Irish roads; 8.3 fatalities occurred for every 100 million miles covered by road vehicles. The comparable figure for scheduled air services is a fatality of 0.5 per 100 million miles flown by passenger aircraft.

The national airline, Aer Lingus, has been in operation since 1936, and has carried a total of 20 million passengers in those 37 years. During all of that time only 77 passengers were lost.

Statistics for the average person are uninteresting and also not immediately available. Here, however, are some facts for the main Irish airports of Cork, Dublin, and Shannon for 1969 and 1970: no passenger fatality or serious incident occurred at any of these places, or anywhere in Ireland during those two years. In that time 5,646,295 people used the airports, and the total take-offs and landings of commercial aircraft came to 115,451.

Statistical records covering all the aspects of civil flying are not compiled too well for the years before 1946. However, aviation received an enormous technical boost after the Second World War, and organisations were formed that provided for international exchange of information, standardisation of procedures, and the establishment of common control and safety regulations. One of such groups is composed of world governments and is called the International Civil Aviation Organisation (ICAO). The statistics available are well compounded and documented, and it is from such records that data has been extracted in a survey of crashes involving public transport aeroplanes and executive jets during the period 1946-71.

ICAO defines an accident as 'An occurrence associated with the operation of an aircraft which takes place between the time any person boards the aircraft with the intention of flight until such time as all such persons have disembarked in which :— (1) Any person suffers death or serious injury as a result of being in or upon the aircraft or by direct contact with the aircraft or anything attached thereto; or (2) The aircraft receives substantial damage.'

There are a number of ways in which an aircraft accident may be analysed and a current method, favoured by investigators in America, is by breakdown and tabulation of each and every factor which has caused or contributed to the incident. This is not to say that in previous occurrences or other administrations such aspects were not fully investigated, but the older system rather pushed the statistics to a greater extent into the human error bracket.

A simple example will illustrate the point. We assume that a twin-engined aeroplane suffered an engine failure in flight, and subsequently crashed on the approach because the pilot lost control. All the technicalities involving the failure of the engine would be examined to find the cause. The weather existing at the time would be considered, together with the runway approach lighting, radio aids, general mechanical state of the aeroplane and pilot physical condition; nothing would be left out of the scrutiny, but in the final analysis the accident could be classified as caused by 'pilot error.'

The new process which the Americans have evolved requires the same thorough investigation, but now the causes of our hypothetical accident would be listed as follows:— Complete failure of No. 4 piston; Poor visibility and icing conditions on the approach; Loss of control of the aircraft due to ice accumulation; or pilot error.

This system is not an attempt to diminish human responsibility, but is an endeavour to examine trends and factors more closely so that accident prevention measures can be improved by informative statistics.

The British Civil Aviation Administration has tabulated by physical cause each accident involving aircraft engaged in civil aviation from 1946 until the present date. The publication is widely circulated and is an invaluable aid to any agency involved in aviation safety standards.

Their classifications are listed here in the order of the total numbers of the accidents (greatest number to least):

Overrunning or veering off runway.
Collision with high ground.
Collision with water.
Inflight fire or smoke.

Major powerplant disruption, or loss of propeller in flight.

Failure of all power units.

Mid air collision.

Third party accidents.

Ice or snow accretion on airframe or engine.

Airframe failure.

Instruments: incorrectly set or misread, failure, malfunction, or design.

Fuel: exhaustion, starvation, or mismanagement.

Electrical system: failure or malfunction.

Doors or windows opening in flight.

Aquaplaning.

Miscellaneous.

Bird strike or ingestion.

Shot at by ground fire, or shot or forced down by fighter aircraft.

Hail damage.

Crew incapacitation.

Cargo breaking loose.

Lightning strike.

Tyre burst after retraction.

* * *

Ireland entered the world of large scale civil aviation in 1946, and I can find no record of any accident involving loss of life on a commercial aeroplane in this country prior to that year. Since that time, however, a total of 258 people have been killed, and 53 injured, in crashes involving Irish or foreign commercial aircraft in Ireland. In accidents to small private aircraft, 19 lives were lost and 15 people injured.

On the day of 12 August 1946, a JU52 trimotor of the Transport Command of the French L'Armee de L'Air was on its way to Dublin with 22 young French girls and four crew members. The weather was cloudy with rain and strong winds. The JU52 struck a hill in the Djouce mountain in Co. Wicklow. The pilot saw the ground through the mist and a few seconds before impact. He pulled the nose of the plane up, and this action saved the aircraft from disintegration, and the occupants from graver injuries. The accident was the direct result of an error of navigation.

In December of that same year, a TWA Lockheed Constellation was making its final approach through low hazy clouds to Shannon Airport. It made a turn and disappeared from sight. There was a sudden flash of fire as the aircraft struck an island one mile from the airport; 13 people were killed and nine seriously injured.

The investigators discovered that an altimeter had given an incorrect reading; this resulted in the pilot conducting his approach at a dangerously low altitude. A further contributory cause was the fogging up of the unheated windshield panels; this restricted the view from the cockpit.

Pan American Flight 1-10, a Lockheed Constellation, was over Shannon on 15 April 1958. The aircraft used the instrument landing system to make an approach to runway 23; it carried out a 'missed approach,' which was observed by the control tower through a break in the clouds. During the second approach the aircraft struck the ground short of the end of the runway. Fire broke out immediately and 20 passengers and 10 crew members perished.

There was one remarkable escape from this disaster; the cabin broke apart with the impact and a man was thrown completely clear of the wreckage, uninjured. He knew his wife was waiting to meet him in the terminal, and he stumbled through mud and water until he reached the runway, and then he ran that mile to the terminal building. His wife had gone by car to the scene of the accident and saw there were no survivors — what a joyous reunion it must have been.

From an analysis of the wreckage no mechanical defect could be found. The pilot's fluorescent instrument panel light had given trouble on the two preceding flights but there were no spares available. The probable cause of the crash was the continuation of the instrument approach to a very low altitude. The failure of the instrument panel fluorescent light may have been a contributory factor.

A KLM Constellation crashed in the river Shannon on the 5 September 1954, killing 28 people; there were 28 survivors. The aircraft was taking off for New York in the early hours of the morning, and everything appeared to be normal up to the lift off point. Some 40 seconds later an accidental ditching was made in the Shannon, just 300 yards from the end of the runway.

The official report gave the probable cause of the accident as failure by the captain to correlate his instrument readings when the flaps were being retracted. This mistake was partly accounted for by the effect on the instrument indications of an inadvertent and unexpected undercarriage re-extension, which affected the aircraft's normal performance.

Two American pilots were delivering a twin engined Convair passenger plane to Swissair in Zurich. An enroute stop was planned at Shannon on the night of 15 July 1956. During a steep turn onto a final approach the plane was seen to drop and strike the ground; it was destroyed by the impact but there was no fire. The four occupants were killed.

One of the possible reasons for the accident was an error of judgement by the pilot during his approach to land; this resulted in a very steep turn during which the aircraft slipped into the ground. Possible contributory factors were lack of visual guidance which would make a steep turn hazardous at a low altitude; it was a very dark night. Pilot fatigue was also considered another factor.

Alitalia's Douglas DC7 made a fuelling stop at Shannon on 26 February 1960. It was on its way to New York. There were 40 passengers and 12 crew on board.

The aircraft crashed immediately after the take-off and was completely burnt out. One steward and 17 passengers survived. The cause of this tragedy was never discovered. It could only be concluded that for some unknown reason the plane lost height in a turn and struck the ground.

The Douglas DC6B of President Airlines was taking off from Shannon for Gander in Newfoundland. Eighty-three people were on board. The aircraft had been told to make a right turn after take-off. However, after becoming airborne the DC6B made a left turn and continued banking until the wings were almost vertical. The machine fell into the river Shannon 2,000 yards from the end of the runway. There were no survivors.

The inquiry decided that the possible reasons for the accident was failure of the captain to control the aircraft due to either a defective blind flying instrument or a fault in his controls. Unsuitable weather, and crew fatigue, were also regarded as contributory causes. This accident occurred during the night of 19 September 1961.

On the morning of 24 March 1968, an Aer Lingus Viscount left Cork Airport for London. It climbed normally to its cruising height of 17,000 feet.

At the boundary of the Irish control area, the air traffic controller directed the flight to change to the London Airways radio frequency. The aircraft called the London controller in the routine way, but some eight seconds later, another garbled radio call came from the Viscount: 'Twelve thousand feet descending, spinning rapidly.' This was the last contact with the flight.

A prolonged and diligent search was carried out by ships and aircraft, but the main wreckage was not located until 5 June; it lay in deep water, two miles from Tuskar Rock.

A considerable amount of the aircraft was recovered; it was pieced together with infinite care, and studied to deduce its inflight structural and mechanical condition.

People in the area at the time of the accident reported splashes in the sea, and some heard the impact. Others gave evidence which suggested that another aircraft or airborne object was in the vicinity at the same time, but this could not be substantiated.

For some undetermined reason the Viscount had gone into a spin or spiral dive, but the pilot had subsequently recovered control. The investigation stated that the recovery manoeuvre could not have been achieved without inflicting some structural deformation on the plane. This would affect the controls.

The evidence given by witnesses of the possible presence of some other aeroplane or airborne object in the area caused the investigators to consider that the Viscount might have been hit by such a machine. The inquiry could not get positive proof to substantiate this theory, but it remains as a possible cause.

Two accidents occurred in Dublin claiming the lives of five crew-members. A Bristol Freighter of Aer Turas crashed at Dublin Airport on 12 June 1967, and a Viscount of Aer Lingus went down near Ashbourne with the loss of an instructor pilot and two trainees.

The International Civil Organisation has this to say about accidents and their investigation:

'Accident investigation is recognised today as one of the fundamental elements of improved safety and accident prevention. Nearly every accident contains

50

evidence which, if correctly identified and assessed, will allow the cause to be ascertained so that corrective action can be undertaken to prevent further accidents from similar causes. Thus the ultimate object of accident investigation and reporting, which is to permit the comparison of many accident reports and to observe what cause factors tend to recur, can be accomplished. These factors can then be clearly identified and brought to the attention of the responsible authorities.

The world wide collection by ICAO of accident reports and aeronautical publications and documents relating to research and development work in the field of aircraft accident investigation, and publication of the material in condensed form, assist States and aeronautical organisations in research work in this field. By stimulating and maintaining continuity of interest in this problem and the dissemination to individuals actively engaged in aviation of information on the actual circumstances leading up to the accident, prevention also contributes to the reduction of accidents.'

The loss of life in events in Ireland is a tragedy for us all, but it makes those of us who work in aviation labour all the more in the endeavour to make the sky a safer place. The arrival of the jet age has caused a remarkable transformation in air safety records, and a very significant reduction in the fatality rate. Engine reliability continues to improve, and the design of automatic electronic equipment and navigation devices allows the pilot to concentrate his attention more in the overall management, and safer operation, of commercial aeroplanes.

Perhaps, in time, the human pilot will be eliminated completely from the flight deck, and the flying machine dispatched to its world wide destinations by the flick of a switch in a downtown office. This conjecture reminds me of the story of one such machine, which transmitted its taped message to its passengers:

'Welcome aboard our supersonic pilotless Flight 115 to Boston and New York. We are flying at 70,000 feet, at 2000 miles per hour. The weather at our destination airports is good, and we will arrive at Boston at 1800 hours local time. We wish you a safe and pleasant flight — a safe and pleasant flight — a safe and pleasant flight a safe and pleasant flight . . .'

* * *

If one were to pick a number of people at random from the highways, the hotels, the bars, the private homes and the institutions of Ireland, a number would be cranks, eccentrics, or aggressive characters. Fortunately the percentage is low, and even then, when such an individual becomes a passenger these dispositions normally remain dormant throughout the flight. My personal encounter with serious disturbances on board an aircraft is very small, and I have no doubt that this experience is representative of that of most of the other pilots. The usual agitation comes from an intoxicated passenger, who generally reacts favourably when confronted by a stern looking face, and four gold bars denoting captain's rank. There have been occasions when an individual had to be physically overpowered and subsequently physically restrained; these are rare. It was ironic that in the one instance in which I was threatened with bodily violence on board an aircraft, my potential assailant was an American police sergeant!

It may well be that such tendencies are subconsciously suppressed by people when they board an aeroplane, because they realise that only the crew of that aeroplane can deliver them safely to their destination. A further deterrent to violence is, that there are very real penalties in law for any interference with a captain during the discharge of his duties in the course of a flight.

The hijacker is the new menace to air safety, and the obscenity of his act, whether it be political or

52

personal, is ironic, since in different circumstances he will expect some aeroplane or some other form of transportation to convey him safely to his destination.

The popular definition of a hijacker was 'one who robs a smuggler of his smuggled goods after the border has been crossed!' Unfortunately this rather quaint meaning has assumed a more sinister connotation in modern times: the word has come to define an air pirate, or a skyjacker. The act is committed for extortion, mental or political reasons, but it is a criminal act against humanity despite the labels under which it masquerades. Scientific preventive measures are perhaps more effective than prosecutions, but it is interesting to note at this point that in the last five years 153 people were brought to trial for unlawful interference with the safety of civil aviation. The sentences given were very severe, and at least two such criminals were executed by firing squad.

The first recorded hijack of an aeroplane occurred in Peru in 1930, and since that time there have been a large number of attempts, some successful and others not. The present wave of hijacking commenced in the late fifties, culminating in a total of 71 such criminal acts in 1972. The International Federation of Air Line Pilots Associations, representing 51,000 pilots from 65 nations, maintains that there must be no sanctuary for the hijacker, and that even the seeking of political asylum must not justify an act of air piracy. World governments for their part, have signed and ratified a number of important treaties relating to anti-hijacking measures; these agreements were made at conventions held in recent years at Tokyo, The Hague and Montreal.

Despite all of these policies, many nations have dragged their feet for their own self centred, diplomatic or business reasons. The ultimate example of this happened a short time ago in the Middle East, when one airliner was shot down and later another forced to land. Here the actions of one of the convention states against two defenceless civil aeroplanes was reminiscent of the law officer turned highway man, when they commanded: 'halt or I fire,' and 'stand and deliver.'

The important conference in Rome held in August of 1973 was so unfruitful that it drew a bitter but justified recrimination from the world's airline pilots. Here is an extract:

'IFALPA, representing civil airline pilots of 65 nations flying the world's airways, is appalled at the lack of progress being made in Rome by the International Civil Aviation Organisation and the diplomatic Conference towards solving the hijacking menace that threatens air commerce. The near month-long meeting now concluding in Rome has been turned into a political forum, where the serious efforts of the delegates who genuinely want to put an end to air terrorism are being thwarted at every turn.

The pilots of the world are deeply angered at the callous attitudes of certain nations that refuse to place the highest value on human life. As those directly responsible for the safety and welfare of their passengers, the airline pilots can no longer tolerate subjecting them to hostile skies.

It is clearly evident, after the dismal failure of the Rome meeting, that the time will come for drastic action on the part of our membership to halt the senseless terror that has inflicted the world. If certain States cannot agree to assure safe air passage for the world's citizens, it is a certainty that the pilots will not deliberately subject their passengers to risk.

IFALPA strongly appeals to the many States now represented in Rome to take further measures in accordance with International Law against those States which do not fulfill their obligations to ensure the safety of the skies.'

Despite these difficulties, progress continues to be

made; but it may well be that in the ultimate it will be the pilots themselves who will finalise the international issue by refusing to fly into any country that does not fully honour its anti-hijacking obligations, and by imposing sanctions against states or airlines that continue to serve the offender.

Many of us have gone through the security checks at different airports; we have seen warning signs and have been directed to go here and not to go there. Other precautions exist, and there are scrutinies we know little of; they are all wearying and time consuming but designed for one purpose — to safeguard the passenger, the aeroplane and the crew.

The sky is there for birds and all humans to wing their way freely across the earth, but some men have made an obscenity of this right to fly, and thus man has had to protect himself against the acts of his fellow 'civilised' beings. Not even the animals have to protect themselves against their own species.

There are a number of large and powerful electronic listening devices permanently beamed into outer space. They are searching for the first sound of radio waves from distant and unknown planets. The moment that 'bleep' comes in on the probe we will know that there is intelligent life out there somewhere, and it will probably be then that humans will stop preying on themselves. An intelligent being or 'thing' from outer space might not understand that on earth the masses suffer from the excesses of the few.

VI

'Julius, bring the master his beer.'

Julius was no Caesar, but a proud Zulu waiter in a small hotel near Johannesburg. He was a handsome man of that African tribe, who had served the army and been a prisoner of war in Germany. The 'master' and his crew were tired after 11 hours flight through the tropical night from Rome to Johannesburg.

Earlier, when the outline of the Tripoli coast had disappeared, our radar sweep picked up nothing for hours but occasional high ground through the Sahara wastes. Overhead the night was alive with stars that I had not seen before; the navigator trapped them in his sextant and transformed their presence into our position and speed.

The smooth passage of the aeroplane was undisturbed by the friendly African night, but what a passage of time was drifting unnoticed underneath: desolate steaming swamp, and profuse jungle full of Negroes, Bedouins, and Europeans; mercenary soldiers, colonists, explorers, witchdoctors; tribal rites and emerging nations. None of this showed up on the radar scope. Only the mind in its memory and imagination could register and retain such peoples, places and happenings. The radar scan picked up the terrain as if it were something of lifeless solidarity, and slowly intruded its reflection down the range scale — one hundred and fifty miles, fifty miles, twenty miles — until the antenna could detect it no longer. It did not matter to the scanner, which was already absorbed in fresh targets at maximum range; again they drifted down the scale in the same mechanised dispassionate manner. Our electronic eye cared nothing for the crocodiles, leopards, lions, elephants, and snakes. It ignored the luxuriant jungle with its croaking swamp frogs and exotic birds. No notice was taken of all those gentle animals which my Susan, and Daphne, and all the children of the world would cuddle and adore.

There was no place on our radar screen for the tribal men or the bare shapely breasts of their women; no place for the naked pickaninnies with their tight curly hair and deep brown eyes; but there was room for the tropical thunderstorms lying across Lagos and Port

Harcourt in Nigeria. The sky ahead erupted with brilliant white flashes and its light threw the thunderheads into isolated relief. We altered the course to avoid the radar echoes, but the energy which they had generated permeated the clouds, and scrawled static across the windshields with fingers that danced on the glass to leave an angry web of electricity behind.

Past the equator the sky to the east had rapidly brightened with a rising orange tint, but the moon still hung there, its bottom dipped in silver. The thunderstorms gave way to a garden of baby cumulus clouds over the Gulf of Guinea, and the light of dawn began to race up the continent as if to make up for the rapidity with which the darkness had fallen.

*　*　*

It was 500 feet above the shores of Loch Lomond that I first met the girl who is now my wife. We were ahead of schedule on a flight to Renfrew in Scotland, and I had taken the DC3 about 20 miles off track to show some of our regulars that famous loch. The view was magnificent, so I called the hostess, a Miss Keegan, to the cockpit to admire the scenery. We had the radio on, not tuned to a direction beacon but to an Irish tenor singing 'Come Back Paddy Reilly.' I gave her the earphones as we flew low over Loch Lomond. The next day it was not quite so romantic; she mistook me for another pilot.

In leafing through the pages of an old log book where I listed the names of my crew, I can see the youthful pretty faces of the girls who were hostesses when I was young: their personality and appearance and some of their perfume is still impressed in those leaves.

In the early days with my airline, there was a small number of pilots and just a few air hostesses. The last flight of any evening was a night stop, and there was a crew of three men — pilot, co-pilot, and radio operator — all chaperoning the single lady. Not unnaturally many of those girls married one of the aircrew, but today, when the airline employs over 500 hostesses, the mind boggles at such a possibility. Some of these girls still marry pilots, but the majority make their choice outside.

In 1939 Aer Lingus purchased a new modern aeroplane for service on the busy route to Liverpool. This involved a completely new concept of passenger comfort, and a cabin attendant was necessary. A girl from the publicity department was chosen for the job, and she wore a black costume with a matching glengarry hat to which she had stitched a pair of pilot wings. She was the airline's first hostess.

The name 'air hostess' was chosen because it signified a social function, and referred to the young woman who tended to the wants of the company's 'guests.' The job itself is often portrayed as being as glamorous and exciting as that of an actress or a fashion model; it may not be quite as exotic, but it is a challenging career which over 1600 Irishwomen have been proud to accept.

The air hostess is the main link between the company and its guests, and the passenger's impressions are to a large extent influenced by the way they have been looked after on board the aircraft. A pretty face and a pleasant smile is an asset to anybody, but in the cabin of an aeroplane it must combine with responsibility, intelligence, tact, resourcefulness, charm and good grooming. A healthy measure of patience and common sense are also attributes which solve many an airborne difficulty.

The hours are irregular, often meaning work on weekends and public holidays, but there is ample time off and wonderful opportunities for shopping in the busy cities of the world. Accommodation is provided in first class hotels and reasonable expenses are paid in the local currency. Due to seasonal fluctuation in business, many girls are able to avail of unpaid winter leave and take up other jobs or go away on long vacations. Because of the concessions available to airline staff, it is possible for the hostess to travel to the most romantic places at a fraction of the normal cost. Good hotels can be obtained in any resort or city at a reduced rate.

During 27 years of commercial flying, I have been keeping my appreciative eye on the brand image of an Irish airline hostess, and I find them generally charming, good looking, helpful and excellent workers. There is a constant turnover as none stay too long in the job; romance always catches up.

Stewards are not employed by Aer Lingus, and indeed many of the airlines who have traditionally engaged them are now discontinuing their services. A passenger makes certain demands in flight — efficiency, courtesy and femininity — and he gets these qualities in the girls who fly as hostesses with Aer Lingus.

Perhaps our national airline is more choosy than others in hiring and training the right girl. I remember some years ago flying with my crew as passengers on an American flight from New York to Chicago. It was a Sunday morning and the aeroplane was practically empty, so my French navigator spent a long time in conversation with a very pretty blonde stewardess. The navigator's accent would rival that of the late Maurice Chevalier, but suddenly she said to him: 'Say, where do you come from, anyway?'

He replied, with a Gallic gesture, 'From ze France of course.'

She placed her hands on her hips as she stood in the aisle and replied: 'Oh, yeah and I'm a Greek!' which to some degree confirms the old American cliché 'coffee, tea or me.'

The Irish airline looks for a girl of reasonable education, with a pleasant disposition and an agreeable appearance. She must have a general concern about the people to whom she will act as hostess. It will later be of considerable financial gain to her if she has a knowledge of French, German, or Italian, although it is not necessary. She must be between 20 and 26 and will be given a seven year contract from the date of employment; this ensures that no girl will be flying beyond the age of 33. In those seven years the hostess may marry and retain her job, and the company makes arrangements for pregnancy leave during this time if it is required.

Aer Lingus employs as many as 600 hostesses during the busy summer. Usually up to 100 leave every year to get married, but the average working life has of late increased from two and a half to just over three years. Unpaid winter leave is shared out equally amongst those who wish to go, and ensures that any girl, married or single, is available at short notice.

The initial four weeks of training are spent in the classroom, where a general introduction is given which covers the organisation of the company and describes the job in detail. A flying instructor outlines the technicalities of the aircraft and covers the rudiments of the theory of flight. Medical training, dress and deportment, grooming, cosmetics and hairdressing are all part of the curriculum. Finally each student is given personal attention by consultant beauticians.

Emergency drills form an important part of the schooling, and evacuation procedures are practised in simulators and in actual aircraft. Ditching drills and the use of the flotation equipment take place at the large indoor pool at Dublin airport.

All of the practical training is realistically recreated in a simulator where hostesses learn the art of serving drinks, snacks and main meal courses, and achieve the psychological know-how, so important in an aeroplane, to make people feel at home. Here too the hostess is introduced to that bewildering world of international currency, crew documentation, customs forms and regulations, landing cards and perhaps most difficult, the management and tally of her bar sales.

No intrusion is made on the private lives of the girls, although lectures are given on standards of behaviour. The 'bunny' image is not favoured, though the hostess is quite at liberty to make dates with whom she wishes. Here however let me destroy the myth of every airline captain having an air hostess as a mistress, or every pilot having it made with one or another of the girls. An Irish aeroplane reflects Irish socicty, and the random factor existing in the air is no different from that on the ground.

The final instruction is in the use of the public address system, after which the fledgling is allowed on the line under supervision. After three months she returns to the classroom for two weeks for a full refresher course and finally the great moment arrives: she is presented with her wings. Each year of her subsequent service she will again return for refresher training.

Prior to her first flight of the day, the air hostess reports to a supervisor who provides special information. VIP's or invalids are mentioned, as are the special services required. There are briefing bulletins to read, and the supervisor checks her grooming and her kit bag.

On the aeroplane she welcomes passengers as guests, seats them comfortably and makes flight announcements in many languages. The special training aids her in expertly dispensing food and drinks, distributing rugs, pillows and reading material, checking safety belts and answering questions. Overseas visitors usually want to know where to stay and what to visit, and young and not so young men often try to make dates. Some will have had too much drink already, and others are uncorking their 'duty-free.' There may be elderly people, families with children, or unaccompanied minors all requiring personal attention. Worst of all, those persistent pilots keep ringing the bell for tea.

When the flight is completed the girl checks in the bar accounts and voyage reports. If she has any personal problems, she may wish to talk them over with a supervisor who has flown many times with her, and who acts as godmother to her and 18 other girls. I would often like to know what that group of 20 is talking about.

The air hostess authoritative system is somewhat similar to that of the pilots, in that there are chief hostesses and seniors. Promotion to these grades is rapid since the number of girls leaving in any one year is considerable. Another interesting aspect of the organisation is that the airlines of the world sponsor and support an annual meeting of all the chief hostesses. Here problems are discussed, and one hostess is selected to act as secretary and circulate information throughout the year.

In the matter of uniforms, it always comes as a surprise to me to find when our air hostesses change into normal clothes that they are possessed of bottoms and busts. It seems as if their formal dress is designed to disguise the female shape, but only because a uniform has to be supplied which would be adaptable for a wide range of figures, shapes and colourings. The outfit has to be fashionable, and yet designed not to date too quickly; it has to be functional because it is the working dress, and I suppose, really, we cannot be treated with bottoms and busts all of the time.

There were women of other countries to whom hostessing did not come easily. Pakistani girls were shy and most conscious of their social position; the ordeal of becoming air hostesses was to many of them a small scale suffragette movement. They came from a society where all menial tasks were performed by a servant, and it was regarded as a social slur if they themselves took employment which involved anything that was normally the work of their maids. These girls did not regard the job of an air hostess in this way, but were up against social taboos long ingrained in them by their parents. Finally they overcame family disapproval to go into the service of their own company but even then were well chaperoned by stewards. They were attractive women, not necessarily all beauties, but very definitely feminine in silken saris and Persian shoes.

Returning on a flight from Karachi, we once stopped in Beirut, the capital city of the Lebanon; that fabled biblical land believed to have been the site of the Garden of Eden. At night the moon came up behind the snow-capped mountain, and bathed the valley in cold still white majesty; myriads of flickering lights in the hills increased to clusters to spread out and mark the outskirts of the city.

We flew from Beirut to Moscow and over Iran, and we looked down on the birthplace of Harum al Rashid Caliph of the Arabian Nights. We crossed the Elburz mountains and over the Caspian Sea into Russia. At Moscow the refuelling hoses were dragged to the aeroplane by trousered and scarfed women of undetectable age. The routine work on the apron and the taxiway was carried out by females as well. In contrast the male customs and immigration officials were smartly dressed in fine cloth with Red Army type caps and boots. They rivalled the appearance of any guards regiment.

There was a pretty girl dexterously manipulating an abacus in the shop in the airport building and she sold in any currency for which she had change in the till. Significantly the labelled prices on the articles were in that well known Russian monetary medium — dollars and cents!

VII

I received a letter some time ago from a clergyman in a poor parish in the east end of London and he asked me to help him, not with money, but with an explanation of the codes and phonetic expressions which he had heard aircraft using at London airport. His hobby was radio, and on the high frequency channels he monitored the chatter which took place between the pilots and air traffic control.

I explained to him that aeroplanes have a language and a slang of their own. They behave and communicate like a huge herd who are constantly in touch with each other and with their controllers. Commercial aircraft in the sky are always in contact with some channel — each carries two or three multi-selection high frequency sets and a high powered voice radio with a range of 2,000 miles or more. The aeroplane itself is in constant communion with earth, and it automatically absorbs continuous information from direction finding beacons and distance measuring stations and translates the data into bearing, speeds and position fixes.

The universal language of civil aviation is English, and the phrases which are used have a common fundamental technical background which make them readily understood in the many circumstances where ordinary conversation would be confusing. The letters of the alphabet are given a simple distinct phonetic, so that the letter A becomes 'Alfa,' B 'Bravo,' C 'Charlie,' and so on. The pilot or the controller uses English phrases but does not say: 'EIAFR, you are cleared to land.' The message is spoken thus: 'Echo India Alfa Foxtrot Roger, you are cleared to land.' If the pilot has difficulty in interpreting the words because of interference the ground operator spells out the message phonetically: 'Foxtrot Roger clear to land: clear to Love — Alfa — November — Delta.' Similarly radio beacons identify themselves clearly either by voice or Morse code.

Each long haul aeroplane has a radio call code differing from its registration letters. This means that it is no longer necessary for pilots to spend long hours monitoring a crackling loudspeaker in case there is a message for them. If the ground-station wishes to contact a particular aeroplane he merely transmits its radio code letters and this signal activates a bell and a flashing light in the cockpit. This is the cue to the fact that there is a call for that plane, and now the crew listens to the receiver.

There are other metallic creatures of space who have much to say but are more circumspect than aeroplanes. An American satellite bleeped its code message back to earth and then listened whilst its Russian counterpart did the same. When both of the formal transmissions were completed one said to the other: 'Ssh! Let's speak German.'

Since a voice channel is always open, there are airborne ears of every nationality tuned in to the slightest whisper or indiscretion. The reaction is devastating when some hapless aviator mixes up the transmission selector and broadcasts his passenger intended message to the sky at large. The variation on this theme is to jerk everybody bolt upright in the cabin in the dead of night by attempting to acknowledge an air traffic control message through the cabin public address system.

Aviation wit often has its own flavour. I once heard somebody say about a particular Irish voice, 'Every time that guy presses the microphone, you can smell the turf.' A German had been called continuously by air traffic control without success when a heavy accent out of the Arctic night said: 'We haf vays of making you talk.' An Indian transmitted a long message to his company about a mechanical fault in the cabin fresh water system, and when he was finished the inevitable eavesdropper intoned, 'well, goodness gracious me.' Sometimes, too, in the lonely night, the routine call to a weather ship would be made in a sexy female voice, and long after the rest of us had flown out of range those coastguard cutter men down below would be exchanging names and making dates with Caroline and Mary-Lou and Mandy.

In the matter of decorative schemes for aeroplanes, each company identifies itself by an emblem, and the combination of colours gave an immediate clue to the country of origin of the airline. The British have a regal tint of blue and gold, the Irish display the shamrock, and there is no confusion about the Hebrew lettering and the Star of David of the Israelis. A Mexican aeroplane has some of the Aztec influence, and the big A proclaims the American. The Indians paint their cabin windows like the artistic flutings of their temples, and the Greeks hang Olympic rings on the tail. An airline from the Bahamas displays a drooping palm tree at the rear. Others spray their aeroplanes different shades. However, when I asked my co-pilot how to tell an Italian aeroplane, he replied, 'By the hair under its wings.'

Many years ago, a cinema proprietor in Galway brought a leaden pear shaped weight up to the barracks in Renmore. It apparently had belonged to the trailing aerial of a low flying Irish military aeroplane and had been deposited, via the glass roof, on a seat beside a patron at a matinee performance. Sometimes too a seat in an aeroplane can cause a completely unexpected reaction. Once a farmer saw the notice over a toilet seat in a small aircraft: 'Do not use over towns or cities.' 'That's it,' said my friend. 'Send it all down on the farmer again.' He, at least, was not transfixed to a similar airborne seat when the pressurisation failed.

Small objects do fall from the sky from time to time,

but the consequences are not serious since the article usually tumbles to earth quite harmlessly in a field or an open space.

'Ler ddiawl maer coesau fowls yr dod O?' If you knew Welsh this would mean, 'Where the hell are all the chicken legs coming from.'

I knew, and so did Captain Ivan B. Hammond, because it was over Caernarvon in Wales that we usually had our lunch on the outbound trip to London. At that time the chicken from the flight kitchen was not at its best, as it had reposed overnight in a cardboard box.

'Hey, Hammy, it's chicken again!' Back went the two sliding windows and out into the slipstream went the legs and their attendant greenery.

'What will I put in my voyage report?' the captain asked.

'Nid O ufern Dai daeth Y coesau fowls ond or nefodd,' I replied. 'It's not from hell them chickens legs come Dai, but from heaven.'

Each nationality gives its own peculiar imprint to humour. I remember a few years ago walking towards the terminal of a German airport and being greeted by a traffic official whom I knew, 'Good day, Captain,' he said, 'and how is the green airline today?' The connotation of the word annoyed me and I replied, 'Fine Hans, and how is the master race?' Later that evening on a flight to France I met an old pilot friend. 'Marc Paul,' I said to him, 'you are a most unusual Frenchman. You neither smoke nor drink.' He replied, 'Zat is so, but I make ze most magnificent baybees.'

A colleague brought a charter flight to America. On arrival most of the all male contingent were the worse for wear, and a coloured mechanic asked: 'Gee, Captain, what are those guys all about?' To which my friend replied, 'Its a charter flight — a management outing.' The mechanic thought for a while and said, 'Man, that country must be sure in bad shape.'

My favourite stories are those of the ageless Irishman who had given all his life to aviation, and who had a fund of original sayings: 'in one ear and out the two;' 'taking the credit for all the blame'; 'engines or no engines she's bloody well going out.' He was a Dublin man and the humour of his county and the inflection of his accent is probably the most captivating in Ireland.

Going into Croydon just after the war, I was making a stilted copybook approach when my captain's strident Dublin voice roared in my ear, 'Get dowen — for God's sake get dowen.' He was right. He knew if you didn't 'get dowen' with the power on low over the houses and ready to chop at the boundary fence, you would go straight through the hedge on the other side of the airfield and come out on the main London road. When I finally reached ground safely back at Dublin, two workmen were bringing stretchers into a classroom for air hostess first aid lectures. I asked them where they were going with the equipment and they replied, 'there's birds in there passin' out with knowledge.'

I always walked down into the cabin during a flight as I felt it is a necessary part of the relationship between the pilot and his passengers and yet, everytime, it evokes the wisecrack, 'Who is flying us now; is it doing it by itself?'

The cabin of today's aeroplane is large, comfortable, and air conditioned, and in the early morning of a long distance flight the half light of the dawn is usually partially obscured by the window blinds; most of the people are asleep but here and there an overhead light is on and a few passengers are reading and smoking unconcernedly. Infants in carry cots relax in those delightful poses of a baby in carefree slumber: the cots are placed near the feet of their exhausted parents and all around are napkins, books, teddybears, holdalls, bottles and bootees. Mother is usually stretched out on the reclining seat with another curly head on her breast for company.

The men are slouched or stretched, shoeless and tieless, and surrounded with pillows and blankets. An elderly man nestles his wife's grey head on his shoulder, and a pair of lovers are entwined in each other's arms. At the back of the cabin the inevitable talkative, half-jarred man in braces and shirtsleeves has a half eaten cigar in one hand and a glass of whiskey in the other, and is bothering the busy hostesses with unwanted talk.

What a shame to jerk them all into wakefulness and reality by an unwonted transmission to Shannon air traffic control.

VIII

The powerful but soft rhythmic whine of the four large engines of an Irish Jumbo jet echo down into those places where many of the brave aeronauts of long ago made their first flights in wicker baskets and cloth balloons. The big metal Boeing, when fully laden, will weigh 710,000 pounds, and its tanks have a capacity for 39,000 gallons of fuel. It flies at 560 miles per hour, and all its controls are hydraulically powered by eight seperate pumps serving four independent systems. The electronics are routed through many computers; and its navigation system is automatic, self directing and absolutely accurate. Two automatic pilots are fitted which are capable of making a completely blind landing.

The air conditioning would rival that of any modern hotel; an auxiliary power unit in the tailplane provides for the full needs of the aeroplane on the ground. Emergency equipment is comprehensive; fire protection devices and circuits are distributed throughout the cockpit, the cabin, and the engines. The birdproof windows are extremely thick and are heated electrically, demisted by hot air, and provided with washers and rain repellent sprays.

The cabin of a Jumbo can carry almost 400 passengers relaxing in armchair comfort in front of four cinema screens with eight track stereo fitted at each seat. The wing span is over 195 feet; in fact as a man said to me, 'It's the only bloody aeroplane I have ever flown in that I can stand up without bumping my head.' But then, of course, he had never flown in the gondola of Mr. Rosseau's balloon, and listened to the drummer boy beat the grenadier's march.

In the *Dublin Journal* of April 1784, Thomas Todd Faulkner printed an account of a spectacular event in Navan, Co. Meath, which took place on the 15th of that month. It was on that day, so long ago, that Ireland entered the air age.

The extract from the paper reads as follows:

'Last Thursday the long expected air balloon was liberated in this town, in the presence of the greatest concourse of people ever assembled here, among whom were many of the first fashion. At half past two, Mr. Rosseau and a drummer boy about ten years old, placed themselves in the gallery, which was composed of oziers, and fixed to a net that covered the balloon, and on cutting the cord it rose perpendicular amidst a profound silence, occasioned by the astonishment at so uncommon a phenomenon. After thirty-nine minutes progress it became totally invisible but we could distinctly hear the drum beat the grenadier's march for fifteen minutes after. At four o'clock it grounded in a field at Rathoath. Mr. Rosseau and the drummer boy arrived here at six o'clock that evening perfectly well except the drummer, who received a small contusion on his head, through his eagerness in leaping from the gallery. At night a splendid ball was given by the burgesses and freemen of the town.

where Mr. Rosseau received the congratulations of a numerous and brilliant company.'

An advertisement in the previous *Dublin Journal* promised the patrons of the Theatre Royal in Smock Alley, 'A Real Air Balloon — invented by the immortal Msr. de Montgolfier, made by Mr. Farrington, and to be filled by Mr. Riddick, under whose direction it is to be floated.' It was 'to bear up Harlequin on the stage, and take him out of view of the audience.'

The same newspaper reported a dramatic occurrence in Cork, also in the month of April:

'Last Saturday evening at six o'clock the air balloon which was launched from a field near Mardyke, at four the same evening, was seen by two men at Cooper's Hill mountain, near Macromp, distance about eight miles. When first they saw it their amazement was very great; one thought it was the devil appearing in the clouds, taking the tub for the infernal's tail; they made to pursue it but to little purpose, as it fell down between two rocks. Then they brought it home and had a number of villagers to see the wonder, but not having any other light to examine its contents they applied a rush made of bog dale so close that a spark fell on it which discharged the inflammable air with such an explosion as to affright all the spectators, and made them conclude it really contained the Devil. One man was burned in the face in a shocking manner, and a woman slightly.'

The next manned ascent by an Irishman was made by Richard Crosbie of Crosbie Park, Co. Wicklow. He ascended from Ranelagh Gardens by a gas filled balloon on 19 January 1785, and alighted safely in Clontarf. Some 27 years later, an Englishman, James Sadler, soared from the grounds of Belvedere House in Dublin and succeeded in drifting across the Irish Sea. The balloon came down off the coast of North Wales, but Sadler was rescued.

In July of 1817 a further attempt was made to cross the Irish Sea by Sadler's son, Windham. He ascended from the barrack square at Portobello and landed in a field at Holyhead. Ireland's first female passenger was a Miss Thompson who made a balloon flight in that year.

The next recorded ascent by an Irishwoman was in June of 1849. A Miss McQuaide of Lurgan Street, Dublin, accompanied Mr. Hampton in the flight of his 'well known beautiful balloon, Erin Go Bragh.' The flight was from the Rotundo Gardens and it lasted for one hour, the balloon making 'a safe and agreeable descent in a field at Kimmage.'

Enthusiasm for aerostatics had varied during the remainder of the nineteenth century, but 1889 was a year of special significance. In September, a Mr. Spencer held his audience spellbound when he leaped from a balloon 2,000 feet above Clonturk Park, Drumcondra, and floated skillfully down by parachute. Six years later, Professor George Francis Fitzgerald of Trinity College built a glider, and contemporary photographs show him coatless, but still wearing his top hat, as he ran across College Park in an unsuccessful attempt to get the contraption airborne.

Harry Ferguson of Belfast was the first Irishman to design, build, and fly his own aeroplane in 1909; on one of his many flights he carried a Miss Rita Marr of Liverpool who became the first aeroplane passenger in Ireland. A Belfast woman was also active in aviation in 1900; her hobby of photographing wild birds had given her an interest in the mechanics of flying. She too designed, constructed, and flew her own machine. The Irish Aero Club was founded about this time, and members organised a highly successful flying display at Leopardstown Racecourse in August of 1910. The following month a Robert Loraine flew a Farman biplane from Holyhead across the Irish Sea, but he came down in the water near Howth Head. It remained for Denys Corbett Wilson, an English resident of Kilkenny, to make the full crossing, and on 22 April 1912, he flew a monoplane from Fishguard in Wales to Enniscorthy, Co. Wexford.

The years of the first great war put an end to private flying in Ireland, and it was not until 1919 that Alcock and Brown arrived dramatically on the bog in Clifden, Co. Galway, after flying a Vickers Vimy, a modified British bomber, from Newfoundland. They were in the air for just over 16 hours and had crossed the ocean at an average speed of 110 miles per hour; after that length of time they still had fuel for another ten hours. Apart from some hair-raising instrument flying and a period of heavy icing, the aeroplane responded magnificently, and already the mechanical reliability of the flying machine was becoming evident. The two engines of the Vimy never faltered on the crossing; the only failure was with the generator on the wireless set, which deprived the pilots of communication.

Charles Lindberg flew the monoplane 'Spirit of St. Louis' from New York to Paris in 1927, and when he aproached the Irish coast he was unsure of his position. He saw some fishing boats out from the Kerry shore, and he throttled back the engine and glided down near the water, shouting at them through the slipstream and pointing with his hand, 'Is this the direction to Ireland?' The fishermen could not hear him, but Lindberg said afterwards, 'I saw the hills of Ireland and knew I had hit Europe on the nose — Ireland is one of the four corners of the world.' He may have mixed his metaphors but not his intuition or his prophesy.

Following the flights of Lindberg, Fitzmaurice, and others, an Australian, Kingsford-Smith, planned to fly a trimotor, the 'Southern Cross' across the Atlantic from Ireland. At first it was decided to take off from Baldonnel, but the hard packed smooth sands of Portmarnock proved more suitable. The 700 horsepower of the Wright Whirlwinds pushed the 'Southern Cross' into the air on Tuesday, 24 June 1930.

The pilots were in a separate compartment from the other two crewmen, with the huge main fuel tank in the cabin dividing them. Each man had coffee, chocolate, and sandwiches, and at one stage the wireless operator quipped to a nearby ship, 'Our coffee is not so good, but the whiskey is Irish and seven years old.'

The navigator of the 'Southern Cross' was an Irishman, Captain Paddy Saul, and like others before him he encountered considerable difficulty in persistent fog banks and subsequently erratic compass indications near the Newfoundland coast. The wireless operator was able to augment Saul's work by obtaining fixes from ships and shore stations. They finally landed at Harbour Grace aerodrome in Newfoundland, after a crossing of 30 hours and 28 minutes.

The decade was an important one for Ireland in civil aviation. In May of 1932 a young American girl, Amelia Earhart, flew a 450 horsepower Lockheed Vega solo from Harbour Grace in Newfoundland to Derry in $13\frac{1}{2}$ hours. Later that year Jim Mollison, also solo, brought a Puss Moth non-stop from Portmarnock Strand to New Brunswick in Canada; and Alan Cobham toured the country the following year with his famous 'flying circus.' Survey and construction work began at Shannon and Dublin, the flying boat base at Foynes was established, and the first firm air link with the new world was made in 1937 when the British Imperial Airways flying boat 'Caledonia' flew from Foynes to Newfoundland in $15\frac{1}{2}$ hours. It met its competitor, a Pan American Sikorsky Clipper, in mid-ocean; the Sikorsky was on its way to Foynes from Newfoundland, a journey of $12\frac{1}{2}$ hours.

Experiments in England were now complete on the

Short Mayo composite: a long distance, heavily laden seaplane which was carried into the air 'piggy back' by a flying boat and then released at a safe speed. The combination left the water at Foynes in 1938 and 'Mercury,' the seaplane, when released, flew a heavy load of mail and freight nonstop to Montreal. The following year inflight refuelling experiments were carried out from Foynes by an Irish aviator, Captain J. C. Kelly-Rogers. The fuel was fed to the flying boat from a converted RAF bomber based at Rineanna, now known as Shannon.

'Canopus,' 'Caledonia,' 'Cassiopeia' and 'Maia' were some of the lovely names of those aeroplanes; and the press at the time referred to them as 'Queen Marys of the air costing well over £40,000.' Today in Ireland we fly 'Jumbo Jets' costing well over £10 million each, and the press of our time refers to them as 'a city in the sky.'

The government had carried out a survey at the Shannon Estuary in 1935 with a view to aviation development, and Colonel Charles Lindberg flew Mr. De Valera over the area the following year. Lindberg was particularly impressed by the potential of a place called Rineanna, or Shannon, in Co. Clare. During August of 1939 a reconnaissance unit from Baldonnel moved down to Rineanna; they were later relieved by a fighter squadron who remained there until the end of the war.

There are the ruins of many castles and large old Irish houses in Clare: perhaps more than in any other county in Ireland. The proximity of the wide and navigable river Shannon brought much prosperity from trade with European countries, and smugglers defied the revenue cutters and ran in Spanish wine and French cognac to grace the table of rich and poor alike. Hunting was good, judging by the amount of wild meats consumed by the lords and ladies who feasted in the castles, of which Bunratty was typical. There was an expanse of marsh at Rineanna renowned for its game: that exact area today is occupied by Shannon Airport. Reclamation of the land required the laying of almost 200 miles of small fireclay drainage pipes to siphon the marshes dry. It was worth all the work, however, as the position occupied by Shannon airport is an extremely favourable one as either a last or a first contact with Europe for trans-Atlantic flights. The weather pattern too, is better than that of most the European airfields.

It was envisaged then that the large flying boats would continue to land on the Shannon but now, instead of disembarking their passengers at Foynes, they would anchor in the suberb seaplane base that was in the course of construction at Rineanna. A semicircular protective wall had already been built out into the river, and a Dutch dredger was used to suck away the sludge which the waters had deposited for centuries. Passengers and cargo were to transfer to landplanes for their journey to Europe. Construction of the basin was almost complete when aircraft designers realised that a flying boat offered very little advantage over a landplane in the event of a forced landing at sea; it was also very heavy and limited in its use since it could only operate from water. Work ceased at the harbour.

I was with a fighter squadron in Rineanna during the war, and on early morning duty we often saw the big Boeing Clippers emerge from a low cloud ceiling on the run down to the water at Foynes. This flying boat had sponsons instead of the usual wing tip floats, and as its lighted cabin windows passed slowly by in the dawn, it looked like a ship floating in midair.

The flying boats were flown by specialist crews who knew the Irish air traffic controllers very well; most of them were fellow army officers. One particular morning the controller was anxious about the water condition, and so had gone out on the estuary half an hour before the aeroplane was due to arrive overhead. Voice communication was primitive, but it existed in the form of a black wooden loudspeaker in the corner of the cabin on the vessel. Matters soon became complicated because the flying boat was having difficulty in understanding the landing information passed from the launch. The captain's voice became testy and he made a provocative remark, to which the control officer answered: 'Who the hell do you think you are talking to?' The black box in the corner crackled the reply: 'You, ya baldy headed auld bastard.'

The vicissitudes of the war brought an occasional stray American bomber on a delivery flight into Shannon for fuel; Ireland provided them with petrol and gave hospitality to the airmen, who were only permitted to remain a maximum of 24 hours. The bombers were delivered by their crews who were to fly them on operations when they reached their units in England.

Many foreign military aircraft crashed in Ireland during the war, but 1944 saw the greatest number; and from the recorded incursions into Irish airspace of Allied and German warplanes during this time, it was surprising that more did not come to grief. The aircraft observation system consisted of a network of strategically placed listening posts. Observers telephoned their information into local centres who correlated and passed it on to headquarters in Clondalkin. Here the reports were analysed to provide the army with accurate intelligence on all aircraft movements over Ireland. The problem of crashing military aircraft became so acute that large white identification numbers were placed at prominent coastal points to enable strays to identify their position; this was of tremendous value to the Allies.

Many of these aeroplanes landed on the bogs as the treacherous surface seemed inviting from the air. A crash crew from Baldonnel found an American fighter intact, but lying over on its back on the soggy moss. The pilot was dead, but ironically he had received no injuries in the forced landing; he had survived the impact only to break his neck against the canopy top when he released his harness straps as he hung upside down.

Many of the aircraft, particularly the fighter bombers, landed in restricted places, and it was impossible to fly them out. Air Corps crews removed guns, bombs, ammunition, and loose equipment. The area was then cordoned off by the army until such time as the machine could be dismantled and loaded on long trailers for the journey to Baldonnel. The neutrality question was a tricky one, but most of the Allied warplanes were brought to the border and handed over to the RAF.

American aircraft did not have the gaunt, purposeful and souless interior of its British and German counterparts. Their cockpits were lined with leatherette, and coffee flasks were fixed to the structure at each crewman's position. The flight decks were finished with the same taste and care as is found in latter day commercial aircraft.

My assigned duty for one of these missions concerned a balloon, not an aeroplane. A forestry worker heard its cable trailing through the trees and, looking skywards, saw what it was attached to. With the help of his companions he wound the cable around a tree trunk, anchored the balloon and rang the army. When we got there, we saw that there was an explosive device hanging some few hundred feet down the cable: with an winch on an armoured car, we contrived to release the deadly contraption, and it drifted out over the Atlantic in an easterly wind.

The driver brought us back to the barracks by way of one of the completed runways, and there, jogging along quite unconcernedly in the opposite direction, was our man with his cart and two large tar barrels. Some of the dry toilet facilities at the camp required the very necessary chore of being cleared out a number of times a week, and the job was done by a local with a horse and cart and two honey barrels. He augmented his pay by selling home made butter, but, as the armoured car driver said, 'He finds it difficult to sell because the lads call it "Shitman's butter".'

Mr. Rosseau never bought butter in Rineanna, and it's a long time since he made the first manned flight over Ireland, but if he were looking down now he would see 136 civil aircraft on the Irish register flown out of 16 licensed aerodromes by a total of 686 pilots, 41 navigators and five flight engineers, and their subsequent manoeuvres in the air would be the business of an an air traffic control staff of over 250 men and women.

Mr. Rosseau, you can be proud you filled that balloon with gas.

*   *   *

The military manoeuvres of August, 1942, ranged over the mountains around the Suir and the Blackwater rivers, and our army co-operation squadron operated from a landing strip near Cashel. I flew a Lysander: a high wing monoplane specifically designed for reconnaissance and army work. The flight commander lost no time in familiarising us with the area, and in the early dawn the flight went out in formation; we skirted the edge of the Galtees and swept down the Blackwater between Fermoy and Lismore.

The valley was still in slumber, and only a random spiral of smoke identified the presence of a unit not yet distinguishable as friend or foe. The morning sun lay low on the horizon, and beamed its slanting rays into the glen, the shafts of light were etched with blue as they filtered down into the misty dampness of the river's environment. Heather patches glistening rocky outcrops, vivid splashes of yellow furze, stunted trees, and all the glorious tinting of changing greens slipped by the large cockpit window as we banked over the mountains away to the south, and went out low over the water at Ballycotton. The winding coast fell rapidly behind us, and I knew that my rear gunner was contemplating the receding shores of his beloved County Cork.

We flew over the sea at 500 feet and the flight commander signalled to open out. My wing mate on the other side came into view and we exchanged greetings, his black identification number glistened in the sun behind the orange and green roundel near the tail. We were all bobbing up and down in the warm air, and the propeller discs were changing and weaving as their spinning blades tossed the sunlight into circular patterns.

Another signal came from the lead aircraft, and I pushed the throttle up to come in tight on the turn and, as the other two tilted below, we turned around and went back to the coast. This time we came in high, climbing up through cotton cloud puffs only to file into line astern as we came diving down on a mountain road. We had caught an enemy column on the move: troop filled lorries, Bren gun carriers and armoured cars deployed in every direction, and before all that chaos had sorted itself out we hugged the Comaragh mountains finally to bump safely across the rough grass surface of our landing field near the foot of Slievenamon.

Six biplanes of No 2 Squadron Royal Flying Corps flew to Ireland in 1913 to carry out exercises with the British army. This was the first operation of military aircraft in this country. There was practically no further activity until the German submarine fleet increased its operations in the Irish sea during the war, but by 1917 the admiralty had established two airship bases: one at Malahide Castle, Co. Dublin. and the other at Johnstown Castle in Co. Wexford.

British engineers had already surveyed possible sites for aerodromes and a young officer, Sholto Douglas, flew over the areas and selected as suitable places Aldergrove at Belfast, Gormanston in Co. Meath, Collinstown (now Dublin Airport), Tallaght, Oranmore, Baldonnel, Fermoy near Cork, and a landing strip at the Curragh Camp in Co. Kildare. Work commenced on the bases in 1917, and the layout was to a standard plan. Aeroplanes from Tallaght now joined the airships in antisubmarine patrol.

American Navy flying boats were based at Cobh, Lough Foyle, Whiddy Island, and Wexford during 1918, and their shore based aircraft operated from Bangor in Co. Down. It is interesting to note that at this time wireless communication was excellent in the flying boats; but to make doubly sure there were carrier pigeons on board!

With the ending of the war most of these places were closed. Flying ceased at Gormanston, and it became an internment camp and the Black and Tan Transport Division base. Baldonnel now was designated HQ of the Irish Wing, RAF.

During the Anglo-Irish treaty negotiations of 1921, two ex-RAF pilots, both Irishmen, were instructed by Michael Collins to purchase a large aircraft to fly him and some delegation members to safety in the event of failure of the talks. The men bought a five seater which was appropriately called 'The Big Fella.' It was never flown for its original purpose, but was shipped to Ireland for use as the first aeroplane of the Irish Army Air Service in 1922. The two ex-RAF pilots became Major-Generals, with McSweeney commanding the Army Air Service, and Russell as both his second in command and Director of Civil Aviation with the Provisional Government. In February of 1922, a lieutenant of the newly established Irish army journeyed to Baldonnel, and formally took over the aerodrome from Bonham-Carter, the Group Captain in command of the No. 2 Squadron Irish Wing, RAF.

A volunteer, who was the first recruit to the Army Air Service, was driven every day to Baldonnel to obtain tools which he stored in an empty hanger. He recalls seeing unserviceable aircraft being burned by Bonham-Carter's men. They also drove lorries over fittings and equipment to prevent them being used again. The British vacated the camp shortly afterwards, but they left it derelict and with all the main gates open.

The Army Air Service became an organised unit in April of that year, and equipping of a squadron began. Six de Havilland 9s, eight Bristol Fighters, four Martin-syde F4s and six Avro 504 K's were eventually added to the 'Big Fella.' It was easier to acquire aeroplanes than pilots, though technicians were readily available. By 1927 the strength of the Air Corps consisted of 26 officers and cadets, and 126 NCO's and men.

The National Army was reorganised in 1924 and the Air Service became a corps. In 1927 Commandant James Fitzmaurice was officer commanding, and in the following year he was invited to crew a Junkers monoplane as co-pilot, with Captain Herman Koehl as pilot and Baron Von Hueneveld as navigator. The single engined 'Bremen' was heavily laden for its crossing of the Atlantic, and a field beside Baldonnel aerodrome was specially prepared as an extension to the grass runway.

In the dawn of 12 April 1928, the 'Bremen' lumbered into the air after a run of 1,000 yards, and was escorted as far as Athlone by an Air Corps biplane. At 0730 hours it passed over Clifden and out into the silence of the Atlantic Ocean. A decision had been made not to carry wireless equipment in favour of extra fuel; as events transpired this was a mistake. If a radio had been on board it would have enabled the 'Bremen' to continue all the way to New York, since adequate fuel was in its tanks nearing Newfoundland. Four hundred miles from that coast the compass failed and the plane drifted blindly up towards Labrador. Had the machine carried a radio, the crew would have been able to obtain continuous position fixes from ships and land stations, and thus continue their flight on into America.

When fog banks cleared, and the Labrador coast gleamed ahead, rather than risk becoming lost again they put the 'Bremen' down on the rough inhospitable surface of Greenly Isle. After a flight of 37 hours the Germans and the Irish had conquered the Atlantic from east to west.

Fitzmaurice did most of the flying, as Captain Koehl was a skilled navigator and he was assisted by Von Huenefeld. The trio made a fascinating contrast. FitzMaurice was young, tall, rugged, and debonair — the perfect adventurer. Koehl was a cheerful, corpulent, easy-going character; and the monocled baron a typical German aristocrat who, despite his infirmity, valiantly made that long and tiring flight.

In that same year the Irish Aero Club was in Baldonnel. Some of its members were prominent public personalities, including Oliver St. John Gogarty. The Baldonnel gliding club was formed in 1934.

In the North of Ireland the RAF maintained bases continuously from the First World War, and these were developed and increased to accommodate bombers, coastal patrol, and fighter aircraft during the second conflict. One of these aerodromes, Aldergrove, is now fully equipped to modern standards and is a main civil airport.

In the 60s the Air Corps was equipped with French Alouette helicopters, and soon their primary role became that of search and rescue, or SAR. These duties are performed in addition to hospital transfers, photographic reconnaissance, aerial survey and army co-operation. Up to the present time the unit has carried out over 200 missions, saving 40 lives. Fuel dumps are located at strategic positions around the country to give the helicopters a greater operating range. The international motto of SAR units is embodied in Gaelic on their flight crest: 'Go Mairidis Beo,' or 'that others may live.'

By 1936 public consciousness had realised that Ireland could and should make a place for herself; a place in the sky amongst the nations of the world. Sean Lemass was then the minister for Industry and Commerce, and he gave enthusiastic support to the founding in that year of a national airline with an authorised capital of £100,000. Aer Lingus was at first associated with Blackpool and West Coast Air Services, who advanced money for the purchase of an aircraft to operate their joint venture: 'Irish Sea Airways.'

The aircraft chosen was a De Havilland twin-engined biplane christened 'Iolar,' and it operated the first commercial air service from Baldonnel in Co. Dublin on 27 May 1936. The 'Iolar' was the 38th aircraft on the Irish register: today there are 136. Five passengers were on board that inaugural flight to Bristol, and they and their aeroplane were attended by 11 ground staff. The mechanical spares for 'Iolar' were kept in a biscuit tin.

The air service proved a success, and was extended to London, with seasonal flights to Liverpool and the Isle of Man. The war restricted development; although a DC3 was delivered in 1940 the company was only permitted to fly to Liverpool airport, with Manchester as an alternate.

The Anglo-Irish Air Agreement signed after the war gave Aer Lingus the sole right to operate and develop services between the two countries: the agreement was amended in 1956 to allow British companies to participate. Route expansion continued with more DC3's, and by 1948 the Irish company was serving London,

Liverpool, Manchester, the Isle of Man, Paris and Amsterdam.

During the year of 1947 a sister company, Aerlinte Eireann, was formed for the purpose of operating trans-atlantic aeroplanes, and that September three Lockheed Constellations were delivered. A number of proving flights were carried out, but by government decree in February of the following year, the operation was suspended and the Constellations sold to BOAC. Aer Lingus itself continued to prosper and expand, and in 1954 the first of the successful Vickers Viscounts were delivered, soon to be followed by twin engined Fokker Friendships. That same year a full scheduled service was opened to Lourdes, and a worldwide reputation was established for the care and attention which the company gave to invalids and pilgrims.

We flew many of these Lourdes services with an aeroplane called the Bristol Wayfarer; an ugly looking machine with a large fuselage, thick high wings, and a fixed undercarriage. It was noisy and unpressurized, but it had a very large cabin which was ideally suited for carrying stretchers. Many of the invalids were mobile and were able to assist the voluntary doctors, nurses, and helpers, in tending to the needs of the incapacitated.

Because the aeroplane was unpressurized we had to fly at low heights, where most of the bad weather existed; but on this day we cruised uneventfully along at 5500 feet down the Wicklow coast and across the mouth of the Bristol Channel, until we approached Dartmoor. Here great heaps of white cumulus and bulky grey cumulonimbus clouds were inextricably mixed. The thunderclouds fanned outwards and up-wards until, at thirty thousand feet, some of them were held steady against the heavens as a great solid head, with fibrous texture at its upper edges. They blocked our way to the south. My co-pilot who was flying, said: 'Tell air traffic control I am climbing to see if we can get through visually; I'm not going through that lot in this yoke with all those invalids.'

Down below in Devon the day had been oppressive, and the echoing distant thunder rolling over the fields had driven cattle together and bunched them close to the shelter near their pasture. On the ground the silence in the countryside became uncanny; even the low swooping and shrill cry of the swallow had ceased. A bee was still in search of honey and the noise of his coming and going was accentuated by the growing absence of other sounds. In time his workings stopped; he sensed the impending downpour and flew hastily back to the safety of his bower, with his wing beat labouring from the weight of the pollen clinging to his tiny body. There was an oppressive silence, a silence you could hear, and the grey low quiet skies were pressing their weight towards the ground. Near the little church at Ashburton, the chestnut trees gathered the first warm, heavy, slow raindrops to drip them down, singly at first; until the tempo increased and the drops hopped back up their silver stems with a light echoing rhythmic patter, as the pools increased beneath the trees to receive them.

The thunderstorm rained and flashed itself out, finally moving away to the south, permitting the familiar sounds to return. The bee was first, and then the swallow, until a sound which grew more compelling and resonated in an echoing expanding way. It was the sound of the two Pegasus engines of a Bristol Way-farer, carrying thirty invalids, two doctors, two voluntary staff helpers, two hostesses, and two pilots. The aeroplane became visible under the billowing grey cloud of the receding storm, and it seemed to hang there; a helpless thing against the challenging sky. After a moment it turned slowly away towards Plymouth, where there was a tiny patch of blue the size of a sailor's breeches. Into this gap sped the aeroplane and the storm broke in fury over Plymouth — but the Wayfarer was gone.

The co-pilot put it down nicely on the uneven paved surface at the enroute stop, Dinard in France. The invalids were carried by Red Cross helpers to a special large dining hall. We went to the wooden building which housed the small restaurant.

There were two notables at Dinard: the customs officer and the bulldozer driver, and they had two things in common; girth and laughter. The customs officer was as formal in his finery as his figure would allow, but the driver wore dark glasses on a suntanned chubby face, an open khaki shirt barely meeting around a great hairy chest, and the smallest pair of shorts in all of France clinging tightly to his big backside.

Wooden tables, red and white squared cloth, crusty bread, a trace of garlic, somebody else's half-corked wine bottle, persistent flies, and the odours of cognac, oil and vinegar, and French cigarettes merged to remind me of what I had seen coming from a collection of French aeroplanes on the day of a rugby international in Dublin. There were mini-skirted girls with tight short hair, busty sweaters, and big bottoms; mini-skirted girls with long hair, flat sweaters, and footballers legs, and girls with cluster necklaces and vivid gashes of lipstick. The men were as varied, with crew cuts and formal lapelless striped suits, fringe haircuts and napoleonic faces, multicoloured jersies and blue jeans. The smell of Gauloises tobacco filled that Irish customs hall, and gesticulating hands, expressive faces, and animated conversation was everywhere.

I summed this up for my co-pilot, adding: 'Can you just imagine the impact that feckin' lot must have had on the boys of Kilalla when the French landed in 1798?': to which he borrowed from a learned Irishman and replied: 'Kilalla yawned and went back to sleep.'

I turned the Wayfarer on to the runway and opened up the power.

From Dinard to Bordeaux the countryside slid slowly by beneath, with only the white puffy clouds born of the glorious day dotting the brownish tint of the earth. There were no radio aids between Bordeaux and the Lourdes airport, and the only way to get there was by map reading. We read the signs like Indians; a railway there, a white tower here, now a valley. Soon we were steady on the inbound radio bearing to the airport at Tarbes, and the swathe in the heavy grass which was the runway loomed ahead.

One did not have to be a believer to find his peace or see it in others in this extraordinary place. Undoubtedly the natural surroundings were in themselves conducive to tranquility of mind; indeed the landscaping and the architecture when combined with the simplicity and contrast of the cave where the apparition took place, produced an intense spiritual feeling. The Gave de Pau flowed turbulently by the wall of the grotto to carry away the glacial waters of the Pyrenees.

The Wayfarer helped the expansion of Aer Lingus into Europe, and Aerlinte Eireann soon recommenced transatlantic flights with Lockheed Constellations leased from Seaboard World Airways. The company eventually purchased its own fleet of three Boeing 720 jets, which were flown very successfully on routes to New York, Boston, Chicago, and Montreal. These aeroplanes were in time replaced by the longer range 707 and in 1971 the fleet was increased with two Boeing 747 'Jumbo Jets.' The Viscounts and Friendships on European flights were replaced by BAC One-Elevens with a final addition of eight twin-engined Boeing 737's.

The name 'Aer Lingus' now covers the complete Atlantic and European operation of a fleet of 18 modern jet aeroplanes. The network covers 30 centres in 12 countries and employs a staff of 5,500. One a a half million passengers are flown annually, and over a million tons of cargo and mail have been carried since 1936. In the last 25 years the airline of that 'Nose of Europe' has increased its gross revenue from £900,000 to a figure of £41 million.

Responsibility is a demanding and varied task master, and in the role of a commercial airline pilot it imposes many commitments, most important of which is bringing all those people safely down from space after having brought them up there in the first instance. The law vests complete accountability on the captain of an aircraft, his is the final responsibility. He must see that an aircraft is fit for service, and that it contains adequate fuel for its journey, with its passengers and cargo distributed correctly. He is legally bound to conduct his aeroplane management according to the regulations which the state has specified, and he must follow the rules of the air although they vary sometimes from country to country.

In terms of social responsibility the problems that compound amongst the 367 passengers in a Jumbo jet all find their way to the cockpit for final solution. In fairness to the flying public there are not many, but like most other pilots, I have dealt with expectant mothers, nervous passengers, drunks, drug addicts, aggressive men, unaccompanied minors, princesses, prime ministers, generals, and politicians with their diplomatic difficulties. I know when the flight deck telephone calls and my cabin supervisor states we have a problem that there is absolutely no point in my wishing it up the stairs and straight out the cockpit window, because there on the coaming panel in front of the captain, stands that invisible Harry Truman sign: 'The buck stops here.'

* * *

Ireland of dreams, of poets and poems, soft colours and soft rain, of great thoughts and maidenly beauty,

Ireland of history; King James and King William, of Sarsfield and Cromwell, of Robert Emmet, and Kevin Barry. Ireland of the farmer, factory worker, financier and soldier; making its way with firm steps into the forefront of world trade and world peace. Ireland: with her aeroplanes winging across the earth.

Is it 30 years since I proudly walked out to my Hurricane fighter, lined up with the others on the apron? We fumbled our feet in the stirrup step and the fitter heaved us up the rest of the way to the cockpit.

Soon groups of three bounced and sped across the grass together, with their undercarriage legs retracting and tucking in grotesquely, as the engines at full throttle clawed the air with fury. Then we were gone, with only a faint ebbing sound reflecting the majesty of our going. Peaceful Irish skies had received us, in contrast to our fellows, who in equally dramatic departures had never come back.

It was years ago since I flew that Hurricane low over the waters of Killary harbour and Leenane. I pulled the fighter into a climbing turn and looked down at Kylemore lake where an artist had painted an enchanting view, and placed a fairy castle there so that mortals could appreciate its loveliness.

Is it that long since I first saw Mossie Quinlan's helmeted head between me and our favourite chimney at Clondalkin? The stack floated into view when the green earth and sky blue had exchanged places. 'OK, we will try a slow roll to the left,' and as we fell out half way around, the drawling voice would sound in the earphones: 'Now I have got her, keep your hands and feet lightly on the controls and follow me whilst we do one to the right.'

I walked those miles slowly up to Baldonnel so long ago and saw the little lazy birds wheeling in the air, but today the aeroplane is not made of fabric and bracing wire and metal longerons. Not now the terrors

90

of heavy icing and the hazards of limited landing aids, not now the open cockpit, the heavy clothing and the swish of the sideslip. Now the vehicle is all metal, moulded and purposeful, thrusting through the skies anywhere, anytime.

Like all those others I went after it, and with it and the miles were consumed and lost on the way; but the milestones of memory remain. Thank you, Mossie Quinlan and Sergeant Spittle.

REFLECTION

Stay but one page longer and reflect with me,
For you and I must part to our separate destiny.
We were all young; youth was ours yesterday, thine today.
Youth was endless, time was too.
Joy was boundless sorrows few.

We had time to see the silver moon and listen to the echoes of a frosty night,
You have time to watch the sun shed golden rays on cloud in flight.
We are all involved, man with machine and machine with man.
Youth is shorter, time is too.
Joy is artificial and sorrows new.

Will they have time to see the silver moon and listen to the echoes of a frosty night?
Will they have time to watch the sun shed golden rays on cloud in flight?
They were all young, but youth is theirs for just a day.
Youth is blighted, time is too.
The machine had won, oh youth will rue.

MORE MERCIER TITLES

GOLA—THE LIFE AND LAST DAYS OF AN ISLAND COMMUNITY

F. H. Aalen and H. Brody

This book describes the geographical setting of Gola and investigates the traditional life and present predicament of the island's community; it attempts to recognise and interpret the diverse forces which have led to the island's decline and to understand why isolated communities in general are almost inevitably doomed to disappear in the modern age.

85342 034 5   *53 illustrations*   128pp   63p

THE STORY OF KILKENNY

R. Wyse Jackson

This is a portrait of a city and of the people who have lived in it: a pageant that includes Dame Alice Kyteler and her coven of witches and warlocks; John Howard, the prison reformer; Bishop Pococke, the eighteenth century scholar and traveller who planted the cedars of Lebanon in the County Meath; Richard Power, who created an amateur theatre in Kilkenny so famous that Grattan and Maria Edgeworth attended it.

85342 391 1   112p   85p

MY STORY (MO SCÉAL FÉIN)

Translated, adapted and annotated by Cyril Ó Céirin

My Story is a valuable document of social history. An tAthair Peadar's lifespan covered the labour of old Ireland in giving birth to the new. It is the story of the nation in miniature and gives the reader an unique insight into the hidden Ireland of 1840-1900.

85342 133 1   192pp.   75p

SIX GENERATIONS
Life and Work in Ireland from 1790
L. M. Cullen
'Overall the book is excellent: there is not a sentence written with which I could disagree. Anyone who wants to understand the sort of life lived by their ancestors should read it, and they will learn much, very enjoyably. It carries a fine varied collection of pictures, closely integrated with the text'. *The Irish Ancestor.*

85342 227 3   120pp.   95p

THE GREAT O'NEILL
Sean O Faolain
First published in 1942 the intervening years have confirmed its standing as a modern classic. For nine years O'Neill resisted English expansion in Ulster and in doing so became one of the most famous soldiers in Europe.

85342 140 4   284pp.   £1.00

THE ULSTER QUESTION 1603-1973
T. W. Moody
This book traces the history of community conflict in Ulster since the early seventeenth century, when a British and protestant colony was planted in a province that had been a Gaelic and catholic stronghold. Intended to establish British power in Ulster on a basis of economic and cultural supremacy over the expropriated native population, the colony by its very success created the polarised society that still characterises Northern Ireland.

85342 399 7   134pp.   £1.50

THE GREAT TYRCONNEL
Sir Charles Petrie
The career of Richard Talbot, Duke of Tyrconnel,
extended from his service in the Confederate Wars of
the 1640s to the aftermath of the Battle of Aughrim
and spans the most turbulent and transitionary phases
of modern Irish history. The book is far more than a
biography: in its re-assessment of Richard Talbot's
career it places a crucial period of Irish history in a
completely new perspective. To the students of history
it is therefore indispensable, while to all those general
readers interested in the evolution of the Irish nation
it presents a lively and compelling account of the events
of one significant chapter in the long story and firmly
establishes its most prominent personality in his right-
ful place as an Irish patriot.
85342 270 2   263pp. *hardcover*   £3.50

THE BEST OF TONE
Edited by Proinsias MacAonghusa and Liam O Reagain
Theobald Wolfe Tone (1763-1798) has been the greatest
single influence on Irish political life. This great human-
ist of protestant birth was the most enlightened Irishman of his day and the story of his short life in Ireland,
USA and France is an amazing tale of incredible
courage, high intelligence, patriotism and adventure.
The best of Irish political thinking has been based on
his writings and philospohy but for a considerable time
these writings have not been readily available.
85342 247 8   192pp.   70p

A GUIDE TO IRISH BIRDS
Christopher Moriarty
An excellent handbook about the birds of Ireland,

giving a description of their appearances and habits and the latest information on where and when they can be seen.

85432 123 4   176pp.   75p

THE ISLANDS OF IRELAND
Thomas H. Mason

Into this book Thomas Mason poured all his love for those isolated parts of Ireland. His keen eye for the unusual in nature, the ancient in man's handywork and his intense feeling for island people emerges strongly from every chapter. This little classic of its kind will be welcomed by all to whom islands spell peace in this world of rush and strain.

85342 123 8   141pp. *illustrated*   75p

THE FAUNA OF IRELAND
Fergus J. O'Rourke

This is the first work of its kind since the publication of William Thompson's *Natural History of Ireland* in the 1850s. This book describes all the amphibious reptiles and land animals known to occur in Ireland but only the more interesting species of birds are described in detail as the Irish Bird Fauna has been dealt with in a number of recent monographs. This book should be of special interest to students and teachers of post-primary zoology and to first year university students. Written with a minimum of technical terms it opens up the fascinating world of Irish Fauna to the interested amateur and average reader.

85342 144 7   176pp. *illustrated*   £1.05

A NATURAL HISTORY OF IRELAND
Christopher Moriarty

This is the first Natural History of Ireland for the beginner—school pupil or adult—who wants a brief outline of the subject. Concentrating on the common plants and animals, the book is divided into two parts, the first part deals with the country as a whole, the second is a county by county guide showing where the animals and plants can be found. English rather the scientific names have been used, and technical terms kept to a minimum.

85342 231 1   192pp. *illustrated*   £1.25

THE YEAR IN IRELAND
Kevin Danaher

This beautiful book describes how the round of the year, with its cycle of festivals and seasonal work was observed in the Ireland of yesterday.

85342 280 X   264pp. *hard cover, illustrated*   £3.50

Send us your name and address if you would like to receive our complete catalogue of books of Irish interest.

THE MERCIER PRESS
4 Bridge Street, Cork
Ireland